Chronology of
British History

BROCKHAMPTON PRESS
LONDON

© 1995 Geddes & Grosset Ltd,
David Dale House, New Lanark, Scotland.

This edition published 1995 by Brockhampton Press, a member of the
Hodder Headline PLC Group.

ISBN 1 86019 068 5

Printed and bound in Slovenia.

Chronology

55 bc

Julius Caesar's first invasion of Britain.

54 bc

Caesar's second invasion of Britain.

ad 43

Roman invasion of Britain began under Aulus Plautius.

Death of Cymbeline (or Cunobelinus), king of the Catuvellauni and ally of the Romans. Succeeded by his son Caractacus who resisted the Romans.

Battle of the Medway: Romans defeated the Britons under Caractacus, king of the Catuvellauni.

First recorded mention of Icknield Way, natural road of Celtic origin from Berkshire Down to the Fens.

47

Construction begun by the Romans of Fosse Way from Lincoln to Exeter as a frontier line against raiding forces.

50

Battle of Shropshire: Romans defeated Britons under Caractacus; Caractacus fled.

51

Romans captured Caractacus.

c.54

Caractacus, English king, died in captivity in Rome.

61

Anglesey conquered by the Romans.

Revolt of the Iceni against the Romans, led by Boudicca (or Boadicea); defeated by Suetonius Paulinus.

62

Boudicca committed suicide by poisoning herself.

c.70

The Iron Age fort of Maiden Castle, Dorset, destroyed.

78

Agricola began his conquest in Britain.

84

Battle of Mons Graupius or Battle of the Grampians: Caledonians defeated by Romans under Agricola; Agricola completed conquest of Britain.

117

Hadrian became emperor of Rome; visited all the provinces of the empire.

126

Hadrian's Wall across northern England from the Solway to the Tyne completed under the governorship of Aulus Platorius Nepos (begun 122).

140

Construction of a Roman theatre at Verulamium (St Albans).
Building of the Antonine Wall from the Forth to the Clyde began.

142

Completion of the Antonine Wall.

166

Construction of the first church in Britain, at Glastonbury.

180

Defeat of the Romans in Caledonia: they retreated behind Hadrian's Wall.

193

Severus Septimius became emperor of Rome (until 211).

197

Battle of Lyons: Clodius Albinus, a rival of Severus Septimius, defeated after ruling in Britain over three years.

210

Severus strengthened Hadrian's Wall across Britain.

211

Death of Severus Septimius at York.

212

Roman citizenship conferred upon all free men.

286

Carausius appointed to protect British shore against Frankish and Saxon pirates; proclaimed himself emperor and recognized.

293

Carausius murdered in Britain by Allectus who became emperor in Britain. Murder of Allectus.

Rebuilding of Hadrian's Wall and York.

303

Church established at St Albans.

304

St Alban the first Christian martyr in Britain.

306

Constantine the Great proclaimed emperor of Rome, on the death of
  his father Constantius at York.

367

Hadrian's Wall overrun by Pictish invasion.

369

Picts repelled.
Repair of Hadrian's Wall.

383

Revolt of Magnus Maximus in Britain; he invaded Gaul and murdered Gratian; treaty between Theodosius and Magnus Maximus,
  leaving the latter in possession of Gaul, Spain and Britain.
Hadrian's Wall again overrun.

394

Consecration of St Ninian as a bishop.

397

St Ninian built a monastery at Whithorn and began to Christianize the
  Picts of Galloway in Scotland.

405

St Patrick began the conversion of the Irish.

407

Revolt of British army: Constantine declared emperor.

410

Sack of Rome by the Goths and withdrawal of legions from Britain.
Edict of Honorius calling upon Britain to defend itself; a provisional
  government set up.

432

Death of St Ninian.

446

'The Groans of the Britons': unsuccessful appeal of the Britons to
  Aetius for help against the invading Saxons.

449
Beginning of invasions by Jutes, Angles and Saxons.
Hengist and Horsa invaded and settled in Kent.

455
Battle of Aylesford or Aegelsthrep: Jutes were victorious over Britons under Vortigern, but the Jutish leader Horsa was killed.

c.463
Death of St Patrick.

477
South Saxons under Aelle settled in England.

495
West Saxons settled in England under Cerdic and Cynric.

500
Scots under Fergus Mor crossed from Ireland to found kingdom of Dalriada in Scotland.

501
Death of Fergus Mor.

516
Battle of Mount Badon: Saxon advance in Britain checked for many years by Britons (possibly under King Arthur).

526
East and Middle Saxons settled in England about this time.

547
English kingdom of Bernicia founded by Ida.

560
Kingdom of Deira founded in Britain by Aella.

563
St Columba landed in Iona to Christianize the Picts of Scotland.

570
St Asaph in north Wales.

575
Synod of Drumceatt in Ireland: Columba got Aidan recognized as independent king of Dalriada.

577
Battle of Deorham: the West Saxons under Ceawlin defeated Britons; Saxon advance resumed.

584

Battle of Fethanleag: Britons defeated by West Saxons.

585

St Columba left Ireland to Christianize Burgundy, etc.

588

The kingdom of Northumbria formed by the union of Bernicia and Deira with Ethelric as its first king.

598

Augustine, sent by Gregory the Great, converted Ethelbert and the kingdom of Kent to Christianity; became first archbishop of Canterbury.

601

Death of St David, patron saint of Wales.

603

Death of St Kentigern or St Mungo, who evangelized the Strathclyde Britons.

Battle of Degsastan: Northumbrians under Tethelfrith defeated Scots under Aidan.

604

Death of St Augustine, first archbishop of Canterbury.

613

Battle of Chester: Northumbrians under Ethelfrith defeated Welsh.

617

Edwin became king of Northumbria (until 633).

***c.*617**

Edinburgh founded by Edwin, king of Northumbria.

626

Penda became king of Mercia.

627

Edwin, king of Northumbria, embraced Christianity under the influence of Paulinus, who became first archbishop of York.

628

Battle of Cirencester: Penda of Mercia defeated the West Saxons.

633

Battle of Heathfield: Edwin overthrown and slain by Penda, heathen king of Mercia, in alliance with Welsh under Caedwalla.

634

Battle of Heavenfield: Oswald defeated Britons and slew Caedwalla and became king of Northumbria.

635

St Aidan went to Holy Island (Lindisfarne) from Iona to re-Christianize Northumbria.

636

Donald Breac, king of Dalriada, invaded Ireland and was beaten at the Battle of Magh Rath.

642

Battle of Maserfeld (Oswestry): Oswald of Northumbria defeated and killed in battle by Penda of Mercia.

Battle of Strathcarron: the Dalriada Scots were defeated by the Strathclyde Britons. Donald Breac, king of Dalriada, was killed.

655

Battle of the Winwaed: Penda of Mercia defeated and slain by the Northumbrians under Oswy.

659

Wulfhere became king of Mercia and restored Mercian power.

664

Synod of Whitby: Oswy of Northumbria decided for Roman against Celtic Christianity.

669

Theodore of Tarsus reached England as archbishop of Canterbury; introduced Greek learning and organized the English Church.

671

Egfrith became king of Northumbria.

673

First synod of clergy held in England at Hertford.

c.680

Death of Caedmon, the father of English poetry.

683

Battle of Glenmarreston: Scots under king of Dalriada defeated invading Angles.

685

Battle of Nechtansmere (20 May): Egfrith of Northumbria defeated and slain by the Picts under Brude; Northumbria never recovered its power.

687

Death of St Cuthbert, bishop of Lindisfarne and apostle of the Lothians.

688

Ine became first great king of Wessex: a lawmaker.

709

Death of St Wilfrid, who had been bishop of York, etc.

713

Aelfwald became king of East Anglia.

717

Church of Iona confirmed to the Roman usage.

731

Completion of the Venerable Bede's *Ecclesiastical History.*

733

Ethelbald of Mercia became overlord of Wessex, etc.

737

Angus MacFergus, king of the Picts, subdued the Scots of Dalriada.

740

Ethelbald of Mercia became overlord of East Anglia.

750

Cynewulf, Anglo-Saxon poet.

752

Battle of Burford: Cuthred of Wessex defeated Ethelbald of Mercia.

756

Strathclyde subdued by Angus the Pictish king and Eadbert of Northumbria.

757

Offa became king of Mercia and made himself overlord of England.

768

Aed Find became king of Scots.

777

Battle of Bensington: Offa of Mercia defeated Cynewulf of Wessex.

778

Death of Aed Find, king of Scots.

784

Construction of Offa's Dyke as a Welsh border defence by Offa.

787

Peter's Pence, the annual offering to the pope, first sent.

793

First Danish raid on Britain, at Lindisfarne.

795

First attack of the Norsemen or Northmen on Ireland.

796

Death of Offa, king of Mercia. He was succeeded by his son Egfrith, who died the same year.

798

The Norsemen ravaged the Isle of Man.

802

Egbert became king of the West Saxons (until 839).
First Norse raid on Iona.

806

The Norsemen desolated Iona.

807

The Norsemen attacked west coast of Ireland.

820

Norse raids on Ireland: beginning of worst period.

824

Iona raided by the Norsemen for the third time.

825

Battle of Gafulford: Egbert of Wessex conquered the West Welsh (in Cornwall).
Battle of Ellandune: Egbert of Wessex defeated Beornwulf of Mercia.
Kent conquered about same time and East Saxons submitted.

829

Egbert of Wessex conquered Mercia.

834

Danish raids in Britain recommenced: Sheppey attacked.

837

Battle of Hengestesdun: Egbert of Wessex defeated a combination of Danes and West Welsh.

838

Norsemen under Thorgils captured Dublin, after desolating much of
Ireland.

839

Ethelwulf became king of Wessex and England.

844

Kenneth I MacAlpin, king of the Scots, became also king of the Picts:
beginning of Scottish kingdom.

845

Malachy I, king of Meath, defeated and slew Thorgils, Norse king of
northern Ireland.

846

Danes defeated in Somerset.

848

Norsemen defeated in Ireland.

851

Danish attack on England under Roric; Canterbury burnt; London
plundered.

Battle of Aclea or Ockley: Ethelwulf of Wessex completely defeated
the Danish invaders.

853

Danes landed in Thanet.

855

Edmund became king of East Anglia (until 870).

Danes wintered in Sheppey.

858

Death of Ethelwulf. His son Ethelbald became king of Wessex and
England.

Kenneth I MacAlpin, king of the Scots. His brother Donald I became
king of Scots.

860

Death of Ethelbald. Ethelbert became king of Wessex and England.

Death of Kenneth I MacAlpin, first king of Scots. Donald became
king of Scots.

Danes under Weland captured Winchester, capital of Wessex; then
defeated.

862

Death of St Swithin, bishop of Winchester.

Aed Finnliath became high king of Ireland.

Death of Donald I, king of Scots. His nephew became king as
  Constantine I.

865

Danes wintered in Thanet.

Death of Ethelbert. Ethelred I became king of Wessex and England.

866

'Great Army' of Danes under Ingwar and Hubba in East Anglia.

867

Danes captured York: Northumbrian kingdom overthrown.

Scotland ravaged by Danes from Ireland under Olaf the White, king
  of Dublin.

868

Battle of Killineery: Aed Finnliath defeated the Norsemen in Ireland.

870

Danes from Northumbria invaded East Anglia; death of St Edmund,
  king of East Anglia, in Battle of Hoxne or Thetford.

Olaf the White from Ireland invaded Strathclyde and took Dumbar-
  ton. Artgal, king of Strathclyde, fled.

871

Danes invaded Wessex; captured Reading; defeated in Battles of
  Englefield and Ashdown by West Saxons under Ethelred supported
  by Alfred; Danes were successful in Battles of Basing and Merton
  against West Saxons; Battle of Marden indecisive.

Death of Ethelred I, king of Wessex, after being wounded at the
  Battle of Merton. His brother became king of Wessex as King
  Alfred (Alfred the Great).

Battle of Wilton: Alfred defeated by the Danes, who wintered in London.

872

Curfew introduced at Oxford by Alfred to reduce fire risks.

874

Danes put an end to the Mercian kingdom.

875

Norse earldom of Orkney established by Harold Haarfager.

Danish attacks on Wessex renewed.

Battle of Dollar: Danish defeat of Constantine I, king of Scots.

Thorstein the Red, son of Olaf the White, conquered a large part of
  Scotland; killed.

Cearbhall, Lord of Ossory, was king of Dublin.

877

Danes divided up Mercia.

Battle of Forgan: Constantine I, king of Scots, defeated and slain by
  Norsemen. Constantine succeeded by his brother Aed.

878

Danes under Guthrum attacked Wessex; Battle of Chippenham
  (January): Guthrum inflicted heavy defeat on King Alfred's Wessex
  army. Alfred was forced to flee.

Battle of Ethandun or Edington: Guthrum defeated by Alfred.

Treaty of Wedmore brought peace between Alfred and the Danes for
  fifteen years; Guthrum baptised as a Christian; England divided
  between the two peoples.

Murder of Aed, king of Scots, possibly by his cousin who became
  joint king with Eocha as Giric I.

886

Alfred recovered London from the Danes.

889

Battle of Dundurn: Giric I killed in battle by Donald II, the first king
  of Scots and Picts.

893

Danish invasion of England under Hastein; Danes defeated at the
  Battles of Farnham and Bemfleet.

895

Alfred the Great captured the Danish fleet.

899

Death of Alfred the Great. His elder son became king of England as
  Edward the Elder.

900

Death of Donald II, king of Scots, in battle against the Norse. His
  cousin became king as Constantine II.

902

Battle of the Holme: Edward the Elder defeated the Danes of
  Northumbria.

904

Constantine II of Scotland expelled the Danes.

910

Danish Invasion of Britain. Battle of Tettenhall (5 August): Edward
the Elder severely defeated the Danes.

911

Danish Invasion of Britain. Battle of Wednesfield: Danes defeated by
West Saxons under Edward the Elder.

916

Edward the Elder and his sister Ethelfled, the Lady of the Mercians,
recovered Eastern Mercia from the Danes.

Battle of Tempsford: Danes heavily defeated by Edward the Elder.

Battle of Maldon: Edward the Elder victorious over the Danes; East
Anglia recovered.

917

Edward the Elder's victories over the Danes continued; death of
Ethelfled.

919

Edward the Elder received the homage of all the northern kings.

924

Death of Edward the Elder. His illegitimate son Elfward became king
of Wessex and Mercia but died within a few months. He was
succeeded by his half-brother Ethelstan (or Athelstan).

937

Battle of Brunanburh: Ethelstan defeated a combination of Scots,
Danes and Northumbrians.

939

Death of Ethelstan. His half-brother became king of the English as
Edmund I (until 946).

943

Malcolm I became king of Scots on the abdication of his cousin,
Constantine II.

***c.*943**

Dunstan became abbot of Glastonbury.

946

Murder of Edmund I by Leofa, an exiled thief. His brother Edred became king of the English (until 955) as Edmund's sons were too young.

947

Erik Bloodaxe, deposed as king of Norway, came to England and seized Northumbria from Edred.

948

Edred suppressed a Northumbrian rebellion led by Erik Bloodaxe.

954

Edred invaded Northumbria and killed Erik Bloodaxe in an ambush. Northumbria given to Oswulf as an earldom.

Malcolm I of Scotland fell in battle; succeeded by Indulf, who made Dunedin (or Edinburgh) Scottish.

955

Death of Edred. His nephew Eadwig (or Edwy) became king of the English.

956

Dunstan exiled by Eadwig. He went to Flanders and Ghent.

957

Renunciation by the Mercians and Northumbrians of Eadwig or Edwy in favour of Edgar, his brother. Eadwig ruled south of the Thames.

959

Death of Eadwig. Edgar became king of the English.
Dunstan recalled.

960

Dunstan became archbishop of Canterbury.

962

Death of Indulf. Dubh, son of Malcolm I, became king of Scots.

966

Murder of Dubh, king of Scots. Cuilean became king.

971

Death of Cuilean, king of Scots, in battle against the Britons of Strathclyde. Kenneth II became king of Scotland.

973

Edgar created 'emperor of Britain' at a ceremony in Bath.

975

Death of Edgar, king of England. His eldest son became king as Edward the Martyr.

978

Murder of Edward the Martyr. His half-brother, Ethelred the Unready, became king of England at the age of ten.

980

Vikings attacked Southampton, Thanet, and Chester.

Battle of Tara: Malachy II, king of Meath, defeated the Danes in Ireland.

Battle of Luncarty: Scots under Kenneth II defeated Danes.

991

Olaf Tryggveson of Norway raided the British Islands (till 994).

Battle of Maldon between the Danes and Anglo-Saxons; Danes were victorious and bought off by Ethelred II the Unready with first payment of Danegeld tax (abolished 1163).

993

Danes sacked Bamburgh.

994

Sweyn Forkbeard and Olaf Tryggveson attacked London but driven off. Ethelred again bought them off.

995

Murder of Kenneth II, king of Scotland. Constantine III (possibly his murderer) became king.

997

Vikings again attacked Wessex.

Murder of Constantine III, king of Scotland, by Kenneth III, who became king and shared the throne with his son, Giric II.

1000

Battle of Glenmama: Malachy II and Brian Boru, Irish rivals, combined and defeated the Danes.

1001

Danes again bought off from Wessex.

1002

Ethelred II married Emma, daughter of Richard, Duke of Normandy.

Massacre of Danes in England on St Brice's Day (13 November).

Brian Boru, king of Munster, became high king of Ireland.

1003

Sweyn Forkbeard again invaded England.

1005

Battle of Monzievaird: Kenneth III and Giric II killed by Kenneth's
cousin, Malcolm, who became king of Scots as Malcolm II.

1007

Danes again bought off from England by Ethelred II.

Ship money first levied in England.

1009

Another Danish invasion of England.

Danes under Sweyn besieged Nairn and defeated Malcolm II at Battle
of Kinloss.

1010

Danes under Sewyn were defeated by Malcolm at Battle of Mortlack
and forced to withdraw..

1012

Ethelred II again bought off Danes.

1013

Sweyn Forkbeard again invaded England; Ethelred II fled to Normandy; Danish conquest.

1014

Death of Sweyn Forkbeard; his son Canute succeeded him. Ethelred
returned to England and began struggle with Canute for the throne.

Battle of Clontarf between the Irish and the Danes (23 April): Danes
heavily defeated by Brian Boru, high king of Ireland, but Brian
himself was killed. He was succeeded as high king by Mael
Sechnaill II.

Sutherland and Caithness came under the control of Malcolm II.

1016

Death of Ethelred II the Unready, king of England. His son Edmund
Ironside chosen as king by Saxons and fought against Canute at
Battles of Pen Selwood and Assandun, or Ashingdon. He was
defeated at Assandun; partition of kingdom arranged, but death of
Edmund left Canute sole king (until 1035).

Malcolm II acquired Strathclyde.

1017

Marriage of Canute and Emma of Normandy, widow of Ethelred II.

1018

Battle of Carham: Malcolm II, king of Scots, annexed Lothian.

1023

Death of Mael Sechnaill II, high king of Ireland. Civil war over the succession led to the end of royal rule in Ireland.

1034

Death of Malcolm II, king of Scots. His grandson became king as Duncan I.

1035

Death of Canute. His illegitimate son, Hardicanute (Harold I Harefoot), became regent while Canute's legitimate son, Harthacanute, was defending Denmark against the Norwegians.

1037

Hardicanute (Harold I Harefoot) became king of the English (until 1040).

1039

Unsuccessful siege of Durham by Duncan I, king of Scots.

1040

Death of Hardicanute (Harold I Harefoot): Harthacanute became king of the English (until 1042).

Duncan I killed by Macbeth, nephew of Malcolm II, who proclaimed himself king of the Scots (until 1057).

Lady Godiva, wife of the Earl of Mercia, rode naked through the streets of Coventry.

1041

The Danish soldier Siward the Strong made Earl of Northumbria.

1042

Death of Harthacanute. His half-brother, Edward the Confessor, son of Ethelred II, became king of the English.

1045

Marriage of Edward the Confessor and Edith, daughter of Godwin, Earl of Wessex.

1051

Fall of Earl Godwin in England because of his anti-Norman views. Edward promised English succession to William, Duke of Normandy.

1052

Earl Godwin's triumphant return.

1053
Death of Earl Godwin. His son Harold became Earl of Wessex.

1054
Scotland invaded by Siward.

Battle of Dunsinane: defeat of Macbeth by Siward, Earl of Northumberland fighting for Malcolm, son of Duncan.

1055
Death of Siward. Tostig became earl of the Northumbrians.

1057
Macbeth killed by Malcolm, son of Duncan, at the Battle of Lumphanan (15 August). Macbeth's step son, Lulach, became king of Scotland.

1058
Lulach ambushed and killed by Malcolm, who became king of Scotland as Malcolm III Canmore.

1065
Revolt against Tostig. Morcar became Earl of the Northumbrians.

Consecration of Westminster Abbey (Collegiate Church of St Peter).

1066
Death of Edward the Confessor (6 January). His brother-in-law, Harold, Earl of Wessex, claimed the throne as Harold II.

Battle of Stamford Bridge (25 September): Harold, king of the English, defeated Norwegian invasion: Harold Hardraade, king of Norway, and Tostig, former earl of the Northumbrians, killed.

Norman Conquest. Battle of Hastings on Senlac Hill between the Normans and the English (14 October):William the Conqueror (William I) victorious and Harold slain: Norman Conquest of England began.

With the conquest the Channel Islands (formerly part of Normandy) became attached to England.

1067
Anglo-Saxon revolt against the Normans crushed.

Work began on the building of the Tower of London.

1069
North of England subdued by William I.

Malcolm III Canmore of Scotland married Margaret of the English royal family.

Malcolm III invaded England.

1070

Revolt by Hereward the Wake against William the Conqueror
(quashed 1071).

Malcolm III again invaded England.

Construction of Canterbury Cathedral began (completed 1495).

1071

Norman conquest of England complete.

1072

William the Conqueror invaded Scotland. Treaty of Abernethy:
Malcolm III of Scotland did homage to William the Conqueror.
Malcolm's son, Duncan, was taken to England as a hostage.

1079

Malcolm III invaded England but was defeated.

New Forest made a royal hunting ground by William the Conqueror.

1086

Preparation of Domesday Book completed (began 1085).

1087

Death of William the Conqueror in France as the result of a fall from
his horse (9 September). His second son William Rufus became
king of England.

1088

Supporters of Robert, elder son of William I, rebelled in Normandy.

1090

William Rufus invaded Normandy and defeated the rebels. The duchy
of Normandy given to Robert in lieu of the English crown.

1089

Completion of building of Worcester Cathedral (began 1084).

1091

Malcolm III Canmore invaded England but was forced to submit to
William Rufus (William II).

1092

William Rufus annexed southern Cumbria to England.

Consecration of Lincoln Cathedral (construction began 1086).

1093

Malcolm III Canmore again invaded England. Battle of Alnwick (13
November): Scots defeated by the English; Malcolm and his eldest

son were killed. Malcolm's brother Donald III Bane became king of Scotland.

Anselm became archbishop of Canterbury.

Construction completed of Winchester Cathedral (began *c.*1079).

1094

Duncan, son of Malcom III, became king of Scotland as Duncan II after overthrowing Donald III Bane; Duncan was killed, and Donald regained the throne.

Construction of Norwich Cathedral began (completed *c.*1150).

1095

Foundation of Durham Cathedral.

1097

Edgar, son of Malcom III, defeated Donald III Bane and imprisoned and blinded him. Edgar became king of Scotland.

Anselm, quarrelling with William Rufus over Church property, left the kingdom.

1098

England invaded Wales to subdue a rebellion.

Magnus Barefoot, king of Norway, invaded Orkneys and Sudreys.

1100

William Rufus shot by an arrow and killed while hunting in the New Forest (2 August). His youngest brother became king of England as Henry I.

Charter of Liberties proclaimed.

Marriage of Henry I and Edith (Matilda), sister of King Edgar of Scotland.

1101

Treaty of Alton: Robert of Normandy recognized his younger brother Henry I as king of England.

1102

Magnus Barefoot, king of Norway, devastated Sudreys and conquered Isle of Man: the Scottish king Edgar recognized his claim to the Western Islands.

1103

Death of Magnus Barefoot.

1104

Building of Gloucester Cathedral completed (begun 1072).

1106

Henry I invaded Normandy and in the Battle of Tinchebrai defeated his brother, Robert of Normandy, and gained the duchy.

1107

Death of Edgar, king of Scots. His brother became king as Alexander I.

1110

Introduction in England of Pipe Rolls, annual rolls for recording exchequer payments, by Roger, bishop of Salisbury.

1114

Marriage of Matilda (Maud), daughter of Henry I, and Henry V, Holy Roman emperor.

1115

Consecration of St Albans Abbey (construction began 1077).

1118

Death of the historian Florence of Worcester.

1119

Battle of Brenneville (Bremule): Louis VI defeated by English.

1120

Sinking of *The White Ship* (25 November): Prince William, Henry I's son, drowned. Empress Matilda (Maud) named as heir.

1123

Foundation of St Bartholomew's Hospital in London by Rahere.

1124

Death of Alexander I, king of Scots. His brother became king as David I (until 1153).

1125

Empress Matilda (Maud) widowed by the death of Henry V, the Holy Roman emperor.

1128

Marriage of Empress Matilda (Maud) and Geoffrey Plantagenet, Count of Anjou.

Holyrood Abbey, Edinburgh, founded by David I.

1132

Fountains Abbey founded by the Cistercians.

1133

Birth of a son (later Henry II) to Geoffrey Plantagenet and Matilda.

First Bartholomew Fair held at West Smithfield London on St
  Bartholomew's Day (24 August) (last held 1855).

1135

Death of Henry I from fever while in France (1 December). His
  nephew Stephen persuaded the archbishop of Canterbury that he
  was the legitimate heir instead of Henry's daughter, Matilda, and
  became king of England.

1136

Stephen subdued baronial revolts.
Melrose Abbey founded by David I.

1138

David I of Scotland invaded England on behalf of Matilda: Battle of
  the Standard, Northallerton (22 August): defeat of the Scots.

1139

Matilda (Maud) landed in England at Arundel and secured a base in
  the West Country, aided by Earl Robert of Gloucester.
Geoffrey of Monmouth's *History of the Britons* in existence: the basis
  of the Arthurian romances.

1141

Battle of Lincoln (February): Matilda captured Stephen; Matilda
  proclaimed queen. Matilda fell out with the Bishop of Winchester
  and besieged him. Stephen's queen, Matilda of Boulogne, besieged
  and defeated Matilda. Stephen was exchanged for Earl Robert of
  Gloucester and crowned king (December).

1142

Matilda besieged at Oxford but escaped.

c.1143

Death of William of Malmesbury, English historian.

1145

Battle of Farringdon: Stephen defeated Matilda.

1148

Matilda left England and returned to Normandy.
Construction completed of Hereford Cathedral (began 1079 on
  Anglo-Saxon crypt).

1152

Louis VII divorced Eleanor of Aquitaine; she married Henry of Anjou
  (later Henry II) and brought Aquitaine to him.

1153

Death of David I, king of Scotland. His grandson, the son of the Earl of Northumberland, became king as Malcolm IV.

Henry of Anjou, son of Matilda (Maud), invaded England. Treaty of Winchester or Wallingford: succession of Henry to the English throne assured.

1154

Death of Stephen (24 October). Henry of Anjou became King of England as Henry II (19 December).

Nicholas Breakspear became pope as Adrian IV, first and only English pope (4 December).

Death of the historian Geoffrey of Monmouth.

1155

Thomas à Becket appointed chancellor of England.

Pope Adrian IV's papal bull, Laudabiliter, gave Henry II the right to invade Ireland.

Wace's *Roman de Brut* completed.

1157

Birth of a third son (later Richard I) to Henry II and Eleanor of Aquitaine (8 September).

Henry II took back from Scotland the territories of Northumberland, Cumberland and Westmoreland.

1158

Somerled expelled the Norse from the Isle of Man and became Lord of the Isles.

Carlisle and Norwich granted charters by Henry II.

1159

Death of Pope Adrian IV (Nicholas Breakspear), the only Englishman to be elected pope (1 September).

1161

Edward the Confessor canonized as St Edward by Pope Alexander III.

1162

Thomas à Becket became archbishop of Canterbury.

1163

Danegeld tax abolished (first levied in 991).

1164

Somerled of the Isles invaded southern Scotland: died at Renfrew.

Royal proclamation of the Constitutions of Clarendon issued.

1165

Death of Malcolm IV. His brother became king of Scotland as
  William the Lion.

1166

Assize of Clarendon. Establishment of trial by jury.

1167

Birth of the sixth and youngest son (later King John) of Henry II and
  Eleanor of Aquitaine (24 December).

1170

Murder of Thomas à Becket, archbishop of Canterbury, by four
  knights acting on the orders of Henry II (29 December).

Invasion of Ireland by Strongbow, Raymond Le Gros and others.
  Waterford and Dublin conquered.

University College, Oxford, in existence by this date.

1171

Henry II landed in Ireland and received submission of many chiefs.

1173

The Princes' Rebellion. Revolt against Henry II by his sons, Henry,
  Richard and Geoffrey. Their supporters were defeated by the king's
  forces at Battle of Fornham St Geneviève.

Canonization of Thomas à Becket.

1174

William the Lion of Scotland mounted an expedition to retrieve
  Northumbria from England and besieged Alnwick Castle. Defeated
  and captured by English; imprisoned at Falaise Castle in Normandy;
  released under Treaty of Falaise on doing homage for his kingdom.

Destruction of Canterbury Cathedral by fire (5 September).

1175

Limerick taken by Raymond Le Gros.

1179

Aberdeen granted charter by William the Lion.

1189

Henry II invaded France: defeated in battle by his son Richard and
  Philip II of France. Henry died thereafter at Tours (6 July). His third
  son became king of England as Richard I, Coeur de Lion.

Legal memory dated from accession of Richard I (1 September).

Independence of Scotland bought back from England by William the
　　Lion for 10,000 marks.

Richard I joined the Third Crusade.

Fire rules drawn up by the City of London.

Office of Lord Mayor of London said to have been founded.

1191

Richard I took Cyprus and sold it to the Templars.

Crusaders under Richard reinforced force besieging Acre (June).
　　Battle of Arsouf (September): Saracen attack under Saladin
　　withstood by Crusaders under Richard I. Richard sailed for England
　　(October).

1192

Pope Celestine III declared the Scottish Church to be independent
　　under Rome.

Agreement between Richard I and Saladin. Richard captured by Duke
　　Leopold of Austria on his way home and handed over to Henry VI,
　　Holy Roman emperor, who demanded a heavy ransom.

1194

Richard I ransomed and released.

Anglo-French Wars. Battle of Freteval: English under Richard I
　　defeated French under Philip II in Normandy.

Portsmouth granted a charter by Richard I.

1197

Anglo-French Wars. Battle of Gisors: Richard I defeated French
　　under Philip II near Paris.

1198

Death of Roderic O'Connor, king of Connaught and last high king of
　　Ireland.

Completion of St David's Cathedral, Wales.

1199

Death in France of Richard I from wounds received in battle (6
　　April). His brother John became king of England.

1200

King John divorced his first wife, Isabel of Gloucester, and married
　　Isabel of Angoulême.

*c.***1200**

The legendary English hero Robin Hood may have lived about now.

1202
France conquered Anjou, Maine, Normandy, etc, from England.
Worcester Cathedral burned (restored 1218).
Death of Eleanor of Aquitaine, widow of Henry II and mother of
   Richard I and John.
Llewelyn ap Iorwerth united kingdom of Gwynedd.
Donnybrook Fair in Ireland licensed by King John.

1205
Walter De Grey became chancellor of England (until 1214).

1206
Stephen Langton nominated as archbishop of Canterbury (until 1228)
   rather than John's preferred candidate.

1207
Birth of a son (later Henry III) to King John (1 October).

1208
Innocent III placed England under interdict (until 1213).
Great Yarmouth granted charter (18 March) by King John.
Liverpool created a borough (28 August).

1209
King John excommunicated.
Construction of first London Bridge completed (begun 1176).
Peace of Norham between England and Scotland.

1213
Cardinal Pandulf arrived in England as commissioner from Pope
   Innocent III. King John surrendered and did homage for his
   kingdom. Papal inderdict lifted.
Parliament called for the first time by King John as an advisory body.

1214
Death of William the Lion, king of Scots. His son became king as
   Alexander II (until 1249).
Battle of Bouvines: Philip of France defeated John of England,
   Emperor Otto IV, etc.

1215
Magna Carta signed and sealed reluctantly by King John (15 June).
   Outbreak of civil war, the Barons' War, when the Pope declared that
   John need not heed the terms of the Magna Carta.
First Lord Mayor's Show in London held.

1216

Barons' War. Louis, heir of the French king, called in by English barons against John because of his failure to honour the terms of the Magna Carta. Louis landed in England (May).

Death of John (19 October): his young son became king of England as Henry III. William Marshall, Earl of Pembroke, became regent.

1217

Barons' War. Fair of Lincoln (20 May): Prince Louis of France defeated.

1218

Restoration of Worcester Cathedral.

*c.*1221

English glass industry established.

1222

Introduction of a poll tax in England.

1224

Death of Cathal O'Connor, king of Connaught, last provincial monarch in Ireland.

1225

English took Gascony.

1226

Waldemar II of Denmark compelled to surrender most of the Danish conquests.

Reputed foundation of St Edmund Hall, Oxford University.

1228

First recorded life assurance bond.

1229

First recorded mention of the Royal Mint.

1231

Cambridge University organized and granted Royal Charter.

1232

Dismissal by Henry III of Hubert de Burgh, his most able adviser.

1234

Marshal Rebellion, led by Richard Marshal, Earl of Pembroke, against Henry III's employment of foreigners in government was defeated (began 1233).

1236

Marriage of Henry III and Eleanor of Provence.

c.1237

William of Lorris composed *The Romaunt of the Rose*.

1238

Consecration of Peterborough Cathedral (building began 1117).

1239

Birth of a son (later Edward I) to Henry III and Eleanor of Provence.

1240

Death of Llewelyn ap Iorwerth, king of Gwynedd. His son Dafydd ap Llywelyn became king.

1242

Anglo-French Wars. Battles of Taillebourg (21 July) and Saintes: Louis IX defeated Henry III of England.

1245

Death of Alexander of Hales, philosopher and theologian.

1246

Death of Dafydd ap Llywelyn, king of Gwynedd. The principality was divided among his nephews.

1247

Foundation of Bedlam (Bethlehem Hospital), London, by Simon Fitzmary.

1248

Charter granted to Oxford University by Henry III.

1249

Death of Alexander II, king of Scots. His eight-year-old son became king as Alexander III.

Margaret, wife of Malcolm III Canmore, canonized.

1250

The Harrowing of Hell: oldest known dramatic work in English.

1251

Marriage of Alexander III, king of Scots, and Margaret, eldest daughter of Henry III of England.

1258

Mad Parliament met in Oxford. Provisions of Oxford forced by barons on Henry III to limit his power.

Consecration of Salisbury Cathedral (building began 1220).

1259

Ratification of the Treaty of Paris (Treaty of Abbeville) (December): peace between Louis IX and Henry III, English claims to several French territories relinquished.

Death of Matthew Paris, English monk and historian.

1261

Henry III renounced the Provisions of Oxford.

1263

Norse Invasion of Scotland. Battle of Largs (2 October): Scots victory; death of Haakon IV (December); succeeded by Magnus VI.

_c._1263

Foundation of Balliol College, Oxford, by John de Baliol.

1264

Barons' War. Battle of Lewes (14 May): Henry III defeated by Simon de Montfort; Mise of Amiens: Louis IX arbitrated between Henry III and the English barons, deciding in favour of former.

First recorded reference to the administrative and judicial post of justice of the peace.

1265

Barons' War. First English Battle of Evesham (4 August): Simon de Montfort defeated and slain by royal army under Prince Edward. End of Barons' War. Restoration of Henry III.

Signature of the Treaty of Shrewsbury, giving recognition of Llewelyn II's overlordship of Wales.

1266

Treaty of Perth: Hebrides and Isle of Man ceded by Norway to Scotland.

1272

Death of Henry III (16 November). His elder son, Prince Edward, returned from the crusades and became king of England as Edward I.

1274

'Little' Battle of Châlons: a tournament between French and English knights that developed into a battle. Edward I nearly killed.

Foundation completed (started 1274) of Merton College, Oxford, by Walter de Merton, bishop of Rochester.

1275

First Statute of Westminster.

Death of Margaret, queen of Alexander III, king of Scots.

1277

Edward I invaded Wales.

1278

Jean de Meun continued *The Romaunt of the Rose* about this date.

Statute of Gloucester decreeing necessity of trial before the granting
of the royal pardon.

1279

John Peckham became archbishop of Canterbury (until 1292).

1282

Hertford College, Oxford, founded (as Hertford Hall).

1283

Annexation of Wales to England by Edward I. Edward secured the
border with England.

1284

Birth of a third son (later Edward II) to Edward I and Eleanor of
Castile (25 April).

Foundation of Peterhouse, Cambridge, by Hugh de Balsham, bishop
of Ely.

1285

Statute of Winchester and Second Statute of Westminster.

First justices of the peace installed in England.

1286

Death of Alexander III, king of Scotland. Margaret, Maid of Norway,
his only grandchild and daughter of Erik, king of Norway, became
queen of Scotland.

1290

Treaty of Brigham between Scotland and Edward I, arranged the
marriage of Margaret, Maid of Norway, and Edward of Caernarvon,
son and heir of Edward I, and the joint rule of the two separate
nations.

Death by drowning of Margaret, Maid of Norway, while on her way
from Norway to Scotland. The Treaty of Brigham was negated, and
there was dispute over the succession.

Death of Eleanor of Castile, wife of Edward I.

Isle of Man came under English government.
Jews expelled from England.

1291

Death of Eleanor of Provence, widow of Henry III.

1292

John Baliol chosen as king of Scotland (until 1296) by Edward I.

1294

Death of Roger Bacon, philosopher and pioneer of science.

1295

Model English Parliament summoned by Edward I.
Edward I invaded France.
Beginning of Franco-Scottish Alliance.
Anglesey conquered by the English.

1296

Edward I invaded Scotland. Wars of Scottish Independence. Battle of
   Dunbar (27 April): Edward I defeated John Baliol; Berwick sacked.
   John Baliol renounced the kingdom of Scotland. Edward I proclaimed king of Scotland. The Stone of Scone (Coronation Stone)
   was taken to Westminster Abbey by Edward I.

1297

Wars of Scottish Independence. Battle of Stirling Bridge or Battle of
   Cambuskenneth (11 September): victory of Sir William Wallace
   over English army as it crossed the River Forth.

1298

Wars of Scottish Independence. Battle of Falkirk between the English
   and Scots (22 July): Edward I defeated Wallace, who was forced to
   flee.

1301

Edward of Caernarvon (later Edward II), son of Edward I, was
   created first Prince of Wales (7 February).

1303

Robert Mannyng's *Handlynge Synne,* an early English poem.
Avoirdupois system of measurement superseded the merchants'
   pound in England.

1305

Betrayal and execution in London of Sir William Wallace (23
   August).

1306
Robert the Bruce crowned king of Scotland.
Wars of Scottish Independence. Battle of Methven (19 June): Scots
  under Bruce defeated by the English.

1307
Death of Edward I near Carlisle (7 July). His son became king of
  England as Edward II (until 1327).
Wars of Scottish Independence. Battle of Loudon Hill (10 May):
  Scots under Bruce defeated English.

1308
Death of Duns Scotus, scholastic philosopher and theologian.
Marriage of Edward II and Isabella of France.
Edward II forced by barons to exile his favourite, Piers Gaveston, but
  Gaveston returned.

1310
Lords Ordainers group of English noblemen came into power (until
  1316).

1311
Edward again forced to exile Gaveston.

1312
Gaveston returned to England and was executed.

1314
Battle of Bannockburn (24 June): English defeated and Scottish
  independence vindicated by Robert the Bruce.
Birth of a son (later Edward III) to Edward II and Isabella (13
  November).
Exeter College, Oxford, founded by Walter de Stapeldon, bishop of
  Exeter.

1316
Edward Bruce became high king of Ireland at the invitation of the
  earl of Tyrone as a counter to Edward II (May).
Conquest of Ireland. Battle of Athenry (August): English defeated the
  O'Connor clan.

1317
Anglo-Scottish Wars. Battle of Inverkeithing: English defeated by
  Scots.

1318

Battle of Dundalk (5 October) between Scots and English in Ireland; Edward Bruce defeated and slain.

Siege of Berwick by Edward II began.

1319

Wars of Scottish Independence. Battle of Chapter of Mitton (20 September): Scots defeated English in Yorkshire; siege of Berwick raised by Edward II.

Completion of St Andrews Cathedral (begun 1159).

1320

The Declaration of Arbroath seeking recognition of the independence of Scotland drawn up by nobles and sent to the Pope, who recognized Robert the Bruce.

1321

Edward II forced by the barons to exile his favourites, Hugh le Despenser and his son, also Hugh.

1322

Battle of Boroughbridge: Edward II defeated his kinsman Thomas of Lancaster.

The Despensers recalled to England by Edward II. The elder Despenser made Earl of Winchester by Edward.

Wars of Scottish Independence. Battle of Byland: Robert the Bruce defeated Edward II.

1323

Truce established between England and Scotland for thirteen years.

1326

Isabella, estranged queen of Edward II, and her lover, Roger Mortimer, arrived in England with an army to overthrow the Despensers.

The Despensers were captured and executed.

First Scottish Parliament (at Cambuskenneth).

Clare College, Cambridge, founded as Union Hall.

Scots College founded in Paris.

Gunpowder known by this date.

Foundation of Oriel College, Oxford, by Edward II.

1327

Edward II deposed by Isabella and Mortimer (January) and murdered

(21 September). His son became king as Edward III. For the remainder of his minority *de facto* power was in the hands of Isabella and Mortimer.

1328

Treaty of Northampton: England recognized the complete independence of Scotland (May).

Marriage of David, son of Robert the Bruce by his second wife, and Joan, sister of Edward III of England (July).

1329

Death of Robert the Bruce from leprosy (7 June). His son became king of Scotland as David II.

1330

Sir James Douglas killed in battle in Spain while carrying the embalmned heart of Robert the Bruce on crusade.

Roger de Mortimer, Earl of March, lover of Queen Isabella, the queen mother, hanged. Isabella was pensioned off.

1332

Edward Baliol invaded Scotland: Battle of Dupplin Moor (12 August): Scottish regent, Earl of Mar, slain. David II fled to France. Edward Baliol crowned king of Scotland at Scone. He accepted Edward III as overlord and fled to Carlisle because of opposition of Scottish lords.

Parliament was divided into the two Houses of Lords and Commons for the first time.

1333

Edward Baliol again invaded Scotland.

Wars of Scottish Independence: Battle of Halidon Hill (19 July): Scots defeated by Edward III.

John de Stratford became archbishop of Canterbury (until 1348).

1335

Edward III invaded Scotland.

Internal free trade established in England.

1336

City of Aberdeen burnt by Edward III.

Clare College, Cambridge, refounded.

1337

Hundred Years' War between France and England began (ended 1453).

1339

Edward Baliol driven from Scotland.

Wars of Scottish Independence. Siege of Dunbar by the English withstood by the Countess of March.

1340

Hundred Years' War. Battle of Sluys (24 June): English naval victory over France.

Edward III claimed throne of France.

*c.*1340

The illuminated Luttrell Psalter produced.

1341

David II returned to Scotland to claim his throne.

Foundation of The Queen's College, Oxford, by Robert de Eglesfield.

1345

Completion of the building of York Minster (began 1291; important additions made *c.*1450).

1346

Anglo-Scottish Wars 'Bishops' War'. Battle of Newburn (28 August): English Northern Levies defeated by Scots under Leslie; Battle of Neville's Cross between the Northern Levies and the Scottish armies (17 October): Scots defeated and David II captured and held in Tower of London.

Hundred Years' War. Siege of English garrison at Aiguillon; abandoned by Duke of Normandy (August); Battle of Crécy (26 August): English victory over French. Siege of Calais began (August).

1347

Hundred Years' War. Battle of Crotoye: French fleet attempting to reach Calais defeated by English; Calais surrendered to the English (4 August).

Foundation of Pembroke College, Cambridge (as House or Hall of Valence-Mary), by Mary de St Paul, the widow of the Earl of Pembroke.

1348

Hundred Years' War. Truce between England and France (until 1350).

The Black Death plague appears in England.

Gonville and Caius College, Cambridge, founded as Gonville Hall by Edmund Gonville (present name assumed 1557).

*c.*1348

The Order of the Garter founded by Edward III: motto 'Honi soit qui mal y pense.

1349

Death of William of Occam, nominalist philospher and supporter of Louis IV against the Pope.

1350

Edward III invaded France.

The Black Death in Scotland.

Dafydd ap Gwilym, greatest of Welsh poets, flourished.

Black Rod first appointed in the House of Lords.

Foundation of Trinity Hall, Cambridge, by William Bateman, bishop of Norwich.

1351

Statute of Labourers attempted to regulate wages and prices at 1340 levels.

1352

Corpus Christi College, Cambridge, founded by the Guilds of Corpus Christi and of the Blessed Virgin Mary.

Death of Laurence Minot, English poet.

1353

Statute of Praemunire.

1356

Hundred Years' War. Battle of Poitiers between the French and the English (19 September): English victory over France won by the Black Prince; King John of France a prisoner.

Burnt Candlemas: Edward III burned every town and village in Lothian.

1357

Treaty of Berwick (October): David II released by Edward III in return for a ransom.

1360

Hundred Years' War. Treaty of Brétigny: truce between England and France. Edward III gained Calais, Guienne, Gascony and Poitou in return for giving up his claim to the French throne.

1361

Marriage of Edward, the Black Prince and Joan of Kent (Fair Maid of Kent).

1362

Appearance of *Piers Plowman*, great English poem, attributed to
   William Langland.

English became language of Parliament and the law courts in
   England.

Quarter sessions established by statute.

1364

Hundred Years' War. Hostilities resumed after death of John of
   France. Battle of Cocherel (May): Navarrese and English force
   defeated by French; Siege of Auray: English besiegers attacked by
   French (27 September) but withstood the attack.

1366

Statute of Kilkenny: English attempt to impose English law in
   Ireland.

Simon Langham became archbishop of Canterbury (until 1368).

1367

Construction of Exeter Cathedral completed (began 1261).

A son (later Richard II) born to the Black Prince (6 January).

A son (later Henry IV) born to John of Gaunt (3 April).

Hundred Years' War. Battle of Navarrete (3 April): the Black Prince
   defeated French and Spanish rebels.

1371

Death of David II. His nephew became the first Stewart king of
   Scotland as Robert II.

1372

Hundred Years' War. English fleet attempting to relieve La Rochelle
   defeated by Spanish fleet (22 June); siege and capture of Chizai by
   French (July).

1376

The Good Parliament.

Death of Edward, the Black Prince.

1377

Death of Edward III (21 June). His grandson became king of England
   as Richard II (22 June). John of Gaunt, his uncle, became regent.

Poll tax imposed in England.

John Wyclif summoned before bishop of London.

Institution of the post of Speaker of the House of Commons.

1379

Poll tax again imposed in England.

Foundation of New College, Oxford, by William of Wykeham.

1380

John Wyclif began to attack doctrine of transubstantiation.

Poll tax imposed in England by Richard II.

1381

First English Navigation Act.

Peasants' Revolt in England under Wat Tyler in protest at the poll tax
of 1380; Tyler killed by the mayor of London (15 June).

Execution of John Ball, English priest and peasants' leader.

1382

Earthquake Council in London condemned Wyclif.

Lollards, church reformers and followers of John Wyclif, active after
now and in the early 15th century.

c.1382-84

Completion of Wyclif's early version of the Bible.

1384

Death of Wyclif.

1386

Charles VI of France declared war against England.

Alliance between England and Portugal confirmed by Treaty of
Windsor.

1387

Barons against Richard II. Battle of Radcot Bridge: forces of the
Lords Appellant under the Earl of Derby (later Henry IV) defeated
the troops of Richard II. The Lords Appellant took control of
government.

Birth of a son (later Henry V) to the Earl of Derby (later Henry IV).

Hundred Years' War. Battle of Margate (24 March): defeat of an
invading French and Castilian fleet by the Earls of Arundel and
Nottingham.

Canterbury Tales of Geoffrey Chaucer were begun (completed 1400).

1388

Wars of Scottish Independence. Battle of Otterburn (Battle of Chevy
Chase) between Scots and English (15 August): Scottish victory
over English under Hotspur.

The Merciless Parliament condemned friends of Richard II to death (February-May).

c.1388
Posthumous completion of Wyclif's later version of the Bible.

1389
Richard II took over government of England.

1390
Death of Robert II of Scotland. Robert III became king. His brother, the duke of Albany, became regent because of the king's physical disability.

1392
Death of Earl of Oxford, court favourite.

1396
Richard II attempted to conquer the west of Ireland.

Fight at the North Inch in Perth between the Clans Chattan and Kay.

Thomas Arundel became archbishop of Canterbury (until 1414).

1397
Richard II took revenge on the Lords Appellant by executing or expelling.

Dick Whittington was Lord Mayor of London.

1398
Duke of Albany forced to resign as regent in Scotland. Regency conferred on David, Duke of Rothesay, eldest son of Robert III.

Richard le Scrope became archbishop of York (until 1405).

1399
Death of John of Gaunt, Duke of Lancaster (3 February). Richard II withheld his inheritance. Richard forced to abdicate (29 September) by Henry IV, son of John of Gaunt, who was chosen king of England by Parliament (30 September). Richard was imprisoned at Pontefract Castle.

1400
Death of Richard II in prison.

Revolt of Owen Glendower in Wales (until 1410).

Death of Geoffrey Chaucer (25 October).

1401
William Sawtrey burned in England for heresy under a new statute,

De Heretico Comburendo, against heretics, particularly Lollards.
Owen Glyndwr began a campaign for independence for Wales.

1402

Death of the Duke of Rothesay in Falkland Palace. Duke of Albany
  recovered the regency.
Anglo-Scottish Wars. Battle of Homildon Hill (September): Scots
  defeated by English under Sir Henry Percy ('Hotspur').

1403

Owen Glendower joined the Percys in revolt against Henry IV. Battle
  of Shrewsbury (21 July): Royalists under Henry IV defeated Sir
  Henry Percy ('Hotspur'); he was killed.

1404

The Parliament of Dunces met at Coventry.
Owen Glendower set up a Welsh parliament.

1405

Insurrection against Henry IV led by the Earl of Nottingham and
  Richard le Scrope, archbishop of York. It was suppressed and
  Scrope executed.
French troops landed in Wales to help Owen Glendower.

1406

James, young son of Robert III, king of Scotland, sent to France to
  escape the intrigues of his uncle, the Duke of Albany. His ship was
  captured by the English off Flamborough Head and he was taken as
  a prisoner to London. Death of Robert III. James proclaimed king as
  James I but not allowed to return to Scotland.

1407

Death of John Gower, English poet.

1408

Earl of Northumberland killed in battle.

1411

Scottish Civil Wars. Battle of Harlaw (24 July): Highlanders under
  Donald, Lord of the Isles, defeated a Lowland force under Earl of
  Mar.
Construction of the Guildhall in London began.

1412

St Andrews University founded.

1413

Death of Henry IV (20 March). His son became king of England as
  Henry V.

1415

Hundred Years' War. Henry V invaded France. Battle of Agincourt
  (25 October): Henry V defeated French but withdrew to Calais.

1416

Hundred Years' War. Battle of the Seine Mouth (15 August): English
  fleet withstood attack by French blockading fleet to get supplies to
  besieged Harfleur.
Death of Owen Glendower, Welsh rebel leader.

1417

Execution by burning of Sir John Oldcastle, leader of the Lollards,
  for heresy.
Henry V took Caen.

1418

Date of earliest known woodcut.
Hundred Years' War. Siege of Rouen laid by Henry V.

1419

Hundred Years' War. Henry V captured Rouen (19 January).
Duke of Burgundy murdered at Montereau; Philip the Good succeeded. Burgundians joined the English.

1420

Death of Andrew of Wyntoun, author of a metrical chronicle of
  Scotland.
Treaty of Troyes: Henry V of England recognized as heir to crown of
  France.

1421

Birth of a son (later Henry VI) to Henry V (6 December).
Battle of Baugé: Scottish victory over English.

1422

The infant Henry VI became king of England on death of Henry V
  from dysentry (31 August) and of France on death of Charles VI;
  Charles VII in France called 'King of Bourges'.
John of Lancaster and Humphrey, Duke of Gloucester, headed a
  council of regency and governed (until 1437).

1423

Hundred Years' War. Battle of Cravant (31 July): Armagnac force
   under the Earl of Buchan defeated by English and Burgundians
   under the Earl of Salisbury.
Treaty of London: freedom of James I of Scotland agreed in return for
   a ransom and hostages.
The Kingis Quair by James I of Scotland.

1424

James I of Scotland set free under the terms of the Treaty of London.
Hundred Years' War. Battle of Verneuil (17 August): English under
   Duke of Bedford defeated the French.

1428

Hundred Years' War. Siege of Orléans begun by English under Duke
   of Bedford (12 October).

1429

Hundred Years' War. Battle of the Herrings or Battle of Rouvray (12
   February): French attack on English defeated; Battle of Patay (18
   June): French under Joan of Arc and Duc d'Alençon defeated the
   English; Joan of Arc entered Orléans (April) and raised siege (7
   May); Charles VII crowned at Rheims.

1431

Joan of Arc burned at Rouen (30 May, canonized 1920).

1436

Charles VII regained Paris.

1437

Henry VI assumed control of government.
James I of Scotland assassinated at Perth by disgruntled nobles and
   descendants of Robert II (20 February). His six-year-old son
   became king as James II.
All Souls' College, Oxford, founded by Henry Chichele.

1441

King's College, Cambridge, founded by Henry VI.

1442

Birth of a son (later Edward IV) to Richard, Duke of York.

1448

French regained Anjou and Maine.
Christ's College, Cambridge, founded by Henry VI (as God's-House).

Foundation of Queens' College, Cambridge, by Queen Margaret of Anjou.

1450

Cade's Rebellion. Rebels led by Jack Cade defeated royal troops at Sevenoaks (18 June), entered London (4 July) but were defeated at London Bridge (5 July). Cade fled and was killed at Heathfield by Sheriff of Kent (12 July).

Hundred Years' War. Battle of Formigny (25 April): English defeated by French: Normandy recovered.

1451

Foundation of Glasgow University.

1452

Birth of a son (later Richard III) to Richard, Duke of York (2 October).

James II of Scotland murdered the Earl of Douglas at Stirling Castle. Scottish Civil War followed.

1453

Hundred Years' War. Battle of Castillon (17 July) English defeated by French in last battle of the War; Bordeaux became French (19 October).

Wars of the Roses. Battle of Stamford Bridge (August), the first battle of the War.

1454

Richard, Duke of York, made Protector because of Henry VI's mental illness.

1455

Duke of York dismissed as Protector and rebelled against Henry VI. Wars of the Roses: First Battle of St Albans (22 May): Yorkist victory under York.

Scottish Civil War. Battle of Arkenholm (12 May): House of Douglas overthrown in Scotland when James II defeated the rebel Douglas brothers; Archibald Douglas was killed in battle, Hugh Douglas captured and James, Earl of Douglas, forced to flee to England.

Appearance of Halley's Comet (named after Edmund Halley).

1457

Birth of a son (later Henry VII) born to Edmund, Earl of Richmond (28 January).

First recorded mention of golf in Scotland.

1458

Magdalen College, Oxford, founded by William of Wayneflete,
bishop of Winchester.

1460

Anglo-Scottish Wars. James II laid siege successfully to the English-
held Roxburgh Castle. James killed by an exploding cannon (3
August). His young son became king of Scotland as James III.

Wars of the Roses. Battle of Northampton (10 July): Lancastrians
under Henry VI defeated by Yorkists under Earl of Warwick; Battle
of Wakefield (30 December): Lancastrian victory over Yorkists
under Richard, Duke of York. Death of the Duke of York.

1461

Wars of the Roses. Battle of Mortimer's Cross (2 February): Yorkist
victory; Second Battle of St Albans (17 February): Lancastrian
victory; Henry VI deposed (5 March) and fled to Scotland; Battle of
Ferrybridge (28 March): Lancastrian victory over Yorkists; Battle of
Towton (29 March): Yorkist victory made Edward IV, son of the
Duke of York, king of England.

1464

Henry VI returned to England.

Wars of the Roses. Battle of Hedgeley Moor (25 April): Lancastrians
defeated by Yorkists; Battle of Hexham (15 May): Yorkist victory
over Lancastrians.

1465

Henry VI imprisoned (until 1470).

Refoundation of Queens' College, Cambridge, by Elizabeth Widville,
consort of Edward IV.

1468

Orkney annexed by default to Scotland.

1469

Shetland annexed to Scotland.

Wars of the Roses. Battle of Edgeworth (26 July): Edward IV's troops
defeated; Edward IV captured (August) and escaped (September).

1470

Henry VI restored as king of England (until 1471).

Wars of the Roses. Battle of Empingham ('Battle of Loosecoat Field')
(12 March): Edward IV defeated rebels under Sir Robert Wells.

1471

Wars of the Roses. Battle of Barnet (14 April): Yorkist victory.
Warwick the Kingmaker killed; Edward IV reclaimed throne; Battle
of Tewkesbury (4 May): Yorkist victory.

Henry VI imprisoned in Tower of London and murdered there (21
May). His son was taken to Brittany for safekeeping.

Orkney and Shetland formally annexed to the Scottish Crown as part
of the dowry of Margaret, daughter of Christian I of Denmark and
wife of James III.

1473

Foundation of St Catherine's College, Cambridge, by Robert
Woodlark, Provost of King's College.

1475

Edward IV invaded France to help Charles the Bold: Treaty of
Pecquigny arranged with Louis XI.

First book printed in English language (*Recuyell of the Histories of
Troye*) by William Caxton at Bruges.

c.1480

Foundation of the Order of the Thistle by James III of Scotland.

1482

Scotland lost Berwick to England.

1483

Death of Edward IV, king of England (9 April). His 12-year-old son
Edward became king as Edward V but reigned for only 77 days. He
and his brother Richard were declared illegitimate by their uncle,
the Duke of Gloucester, who had been appointed Protector of the
kingdom by Edward IV and who took the throne as Richard III (26
June). Edward IV and Richard, the Princes in the Tower, disap-
peared, probably murdered in the Tower at their uncle's instigation.

Rebellion by Duke of Buckingham against Richard III crushed.

1484

Council of the North established to govern the north of England.

Introduction of bail for defendants in legal courts.

English first used for parliamntary statutes.

1485

Battle of Bosworth (22 August): Richard III defeated and killed.
Henry VII became king of England, first of the Tudor dynasty.

Formation of the Yeomen of the Guard.

The *Morte d 'Arthur* by Sir Thomas Malory printed by Caxton.

Cardinal John Morton became archbishop of Canterbury (until 1500).

1486

Marriage of Henry VII and Elizabeth, daughter of Edward IV, uniting
the Houses of York and Lancaster.

1487

Revolt of Lambert Simnel against Henry VII by pretending to be
Edward Plantagenet, son of the Duke of Clarence; Battle of Stoke
(16 June): royal troops under Henry VII defeated rebels under Earl
of Lincoln.

1488

Barons' Rebellion. Battle of Sauchieburn (18 June): death of James
III of Scotland at the hands of rebel nobles, led by his son, James,
and accession of James as James IV.

1491

Birth of a second son (later Henry VIII) to Henry VII.

France obtained Brittany by marriage.

1493

End of the Lordship of the Isles. James IV assumed the title.

1494

Lollards of Kyle in Scotland, pioneers of Reformation.

Sir Edward Poynings became Lord Deputy of Ireland.

1495

Introduction in Ireland of Poynings' Law to regulate Irish government by Sir Edward Poynings: Parliament of Ireland made entirely
dependent on that of England.

Play of *Everyman* not later than this date.

Canterbury Cathedral completed.

King's College, Aberdeen, founded by Bishop William Elphinstone as
St Mary's College (renamed in honour of James IV).

1496

First of several fruitless invasions of England and Ireland by Perkin
Warbeck, who claimed to be Richard, Duke of York, the younger of
the two Princes in the Tower, and claimant to Henry VII's throne.

Magnus Intercursus: a commercial treaty between England and
Netherlands.

Jesus College, Cambridge, founded by John Alcock, bishop of Ely.

1497

The Scottish Parliament passed education legislation.

Capture of Perkin Warbeck after an attempt on Cornwall (October).
  He was confined in the Tower of London.

Killing of Sir James Ormonde ('Black James'), Lord Treasurer of
  Ireland.

John Cabot discovered Labrador, Newfoundland and South Carolina.

Royal tennis played in England by Henry VII.

1498

Erasmus at Oxford.

Building of Holyrood Palace, Edinburgh, began.

1499

Execution by hanging of Perkin Warbeck (23 November).

1500

Death of Robert Henryson, Scottish poet.

1503

Marriage of James IV of Scotland and Margaret Tudor, daughter of
  Henry VII of England.

1504

William Warham became archbishop of Canterbury.

1505

Christ's College, Cambridge, refounded and enlarged by Lady
  Margaret Beaufort.

1507

First printing press in Scotland set up in Edinburgh by Andrew
  Myllar.

1509

Death of Henry VII (21 April): his second son succeeded him as
  Henry VIII, king of England.

Marriage of Henry VIII and Catherine of Aragon, widow of Henry's
  brother, Prince Arthur (11 June).

Gentlemen-at-Arms established as the sovereign's personal body-
  guard by Henry VIII.

1510

Erasmus began lecturing on Greek at Cambridge University.

1511

Holy League of Pope, Venice, and Spain: joined by Henry VIII.

Foundation of St John's College, Cambridge, by Lady Margaret,
  Countess of Richmond and Derby.

1512

Admiralty founded.

1513

Anglo-French Wars. Battle of Guinegate or Battle of the Spurs (16
  August): English under Henry VIII defeated French.

Anglo-Scottish Wars. Battle of Flodden (9 September): English
  victory over Scots: James IV killed; his young son became James V,
  king of Scotland.

1514

Greek New Testament of Erasmus.

First Charter granted to Trinity House by Henry VIII.

1515

Cardinal Wolsey became Lord Chancellor of England.

1516

Birth of a daughter (later Mary I) to Henry VIII and Catherine of
  Aragon (18 February).

Corpus Christi College, Oxford, founded by Richard Foxe.

Publication of *Utopia* by Sir Thomas More.

1517

Treaty of Rouen between Scotland and France.

The Royal College of Physicians founded by Thomas Linacre.

The Reformation started by Martin Luther.

1520

Field of the Cloth of Gold: conference between Henry VIII and
  Francis I of France (6 June).

1521

Henry VIII created Defender of the Faith by Pope Leo X for answer-
  ing Luther.

1522

Treaty of Windsor: between Charles V and Henry VIII.

1523

Duke of Suffolk invaded France.

First recorded insurance policy.

1524

Protestantism banned in Scotland.

1525

Peace between England and France.

Christ Church, Oxford, founded.

William Tyndale's translation of the New Testament completed in
  Germany.

1526

Building of Fountains Abbey completed.

1527

Alliance between Henry VIII and Francis I.

1528

England and France declared war against the Empire.

Patrick Hamilton burned for heresy in Scotland.

1529

Peace of Cambrai ('Ladies' Peace'): between Francis I, the Emperor,
  and England.

Henry VIII's divorce trail began: transferred to Rome by the Pope.

Fall of Cardinal Wolsey: Sir Thomas More became Lord Chancellor
  (until 1533).

1530

Death of Cardinal Wolsey on his way to the Tower of London (29
  November).

1531

Murder of James Inglis, abbot of Culross.

Appearance of Halley's Comet (named after Edmund Halley).

1532

Resignationof Sir Thomas More as Chancellor.

'Submission of the Clergy' to Henry VIII in England.

The Court of Session, central court of civil justice, established by
  James V in Scotland.

1533

Thomas Cranmer became archbishop of Canterbury.

Secret marriage of Henry VIII and Anne Boleyn (25 January); Anne
  Boleyn publicly named queen of Henry VIII; Cranmer declared
  Catherine of Aragon's marriage null; Anne Boleyn crowned; Henry
  VIII excommunicated by Pope.

Birth of a daughter (later Elizabeth I) to Henry VIII and Anne Boleyn.
Thomas Cromwell became chief minister.
Completion of St James's Palace (begun 1532) by Henry VIII.

1534

Act of Supremacy in England (17 November) separating Anglican
   Church from the Catholic Church, signed by Henry VIII, who
   became Supreme Head of the English Church.
Peter's Pence, the annual offering to the pope, abolished.

1535

Execution by beheading of Bishop Fisher and Sir Thomas More (6 July).
Henry VIII declared deposed by Pope Paul III in the first Bull of
   Deposition.
Publication of the English Bible of Miles Coverdale (first complete
   one).
Thomas Cromwell became Vicar-General for Henry VIII.

1536

First Act for dissolution of monasteries in England.
Anne Boleyn beheaded for adultery (19 May); Henry VIII married
   Jane Seymour (30 May); Jane Seymour proclaimed queen.
Pilgrimage of Grace, Yorkshire insurrection under Robert Aske and
   John Pickering.
William Tyndale burned for heresy in the Netherlands (6 October).
Lincolnshire Insurrection against religious and fiscal oppression
   (suppressed 1536-37).
Death of Catherine of Aragon (7 January).

1537

Birth of a son (later Edward VI) to Henry VIII and Jane Seymour.
Robert Aske and John Pickering, leaders of the Pilgrimage of Grace,
   executed.

1538

Marriage of James IV of Scotland and Mary of Lorraine, daughter of
   the Duke of Guise.

1539

Act of the Six Articles against heresy in England.

1540

Anne of Cleves married (January) and divorced (July) by Henry VIII.
Thomas Cromwell beheaded.

Marriage of Henry VIII and Catherine Howard, his fifth wife.
First recorded horse racing event in Britain (9 February) at Chester.

*c.*1540

Apricots first planted in England around this time.

1541

Henry VIII given the title 'King of Ireland' by the Irish Parliament.
Execution of Margaret Pole, Countess of Salisbury, mother of
  Reginald Pole, at the order of Henry VIII.

1542

Anglo-Scottish Wars. Battle of Solway Moss (14 December): English
  defeated Scots.
Death of James V: his infant daughter Mary Stewart became queen of
  Scotland as Mary Queen of Scots: Earl of Arran Regent.
Catherine Howard, fifth wife of Henry VIII, beheaded for adultery
  (13 February).
Magdelene College, Cambridge, founded.

1543

Betrothal of the infant Mary of Scotland to Edward, son and heir of
  Henry VIII; repudiated by Scots.
Catherine Parr became sixth wife of Henry VIII (12 July).

1544

The 'Rough Wooing': English troops under the Earl of Hertford
  invaded Scotland; Edinburgh burned.
Peace of Crépy: between Emperor, England, and France. Title of
  Defender of the Faith for Henry VIII continued by Parliament.

1545

The 'Rough Wooing'. Battle of Ancrum Moor (17 February): Scottish
  victory over English.
The *Mary Rose* sank in the Solent (19 July, raised 1982).

1546

George Wishart burned as a heretic in Scotland.
Cardinal Beaton murdered to avenge Wishart and St Andrews Castle
  captured.
Anne Askew tortured and burned for heresy in London.
Foundation of Trinity College, Cambridge, by Henry VIII.

1547

Brittany united to the French kingdom.

Death of Henry VIII (28 January): Edward VI became king of
England (until 1553): Earl of Hertford (created Duke of Somerset)
became Protector of the realm.

Somerset repealed the English laws against heresy.

Earl of Surrey executed for treason.

The 'Rough Wooing'. Battle of Pinkie (10 September): English under
Somerset victorious over Scots under Huntly; English took Edinburgh.
Capitulation of St Andrews: John Knox a French galley slave.

Marriage of Lord Seymour and Catherine Parr, widow of Henry VIII.

English replaced Latin in English Church services.

1548

Mary Queen of Scots sent to France.

Death of Catherine Parr in childbirth (7 September).

1549

First Book of Common Prayer sanctioned by Parliament and
published (9 June): the wedding ring finger changed from right
hand to left.

First Act of Uniformity in England made the Catholic mass illegal.

Somerset as social reformer: Enclosures Commission appointed.

Ket's Rebellion in eastern England over land enclosures, led by Robert
Kett, suppressed by royal troops at Battle of Duffindale; Kett hanged.

Arundel's Rebellion. Battle of Farrington Bridge (27 July): rebels
defeated by royal troops; Battle of St Mary's Clyst (4 August): rebel
attack on royal army defeated; Arundel abandoned siege of Exeter;
Battle of Sampford Courtney (17 August): rebels under Arundel
finally defeated.

France declared war against England.

Imprisonment of Somerset: Warwick (later Duke of Northumberland)
in power as Protector.

Execution of Lord Seymour, brother of Somerset, for treason in
seeking to marry Elizabeth.

Parliament declared enclosures legal.

The Anabaptist religious movement (founded 1522) reached England.

1550

Persecution of Catholics and heretics in England.

Anglo-French Wars. Battle of Jersey: French fleet besieging St Helier
defeated by English.

Peace between France and England: Boulogne given back to France.

1552

Somerset executed.

Second Act of Uniformity in England.

Second Book of Common Prayer published.

1553

Death of Edward VI from tuberculosis (6 July): Lady Jane Grey, great-niece of Henry VIII and daughter-in-law of the Earl of Northumberland, proclaimed queen by Northumberland but recognized only by King's Lynn and Berwick; Mary Tudor also proclaimed; Northumberland executed and Mary proclaimed as Mary I.

Sir Hugh Willoughby and Richard Chancellor set out in search of northeast passage: former lost: latter found the White Sea and Archangel Passage.

1554

Wyatt's Rebellion. Announcement of Mary I's intention to marry Philip of Spain provoked a rebellion in Kent led by Sir Thomas Wyatt. Insurgents defeated at Wrotham Heath (January); Wyatt executed.

Execution by beheading of Lady Jane Grey and her husband, Lord Guildford Dudley (12 February).

Mary of Guise became regent of Scotland.

Mary Tudor married Philip, heir of Charles V.

Cardinal Reginald Pole arrived in England: Parliament decided in favour of returning to the old religion.

1555

John Rogers burned for heresy in England; many others followed.

Bishop Latimer and Bishop Ridley of London burned at the stake in England for heresey (16 October).

Foundation of St John's College, Oxford.

Foundation of Trinity College, Oxford, by Sir Thomas Pope.

Muscovy Company founded by Richard Chancellor to trade with Russia.

1556

Death of Nicholas Udall, author of the comedy *Ralph Roister Doister*.

Thomas Cranmer, archbishop of Canterbury, burned at the stake for heresy (21 March). Cardinal Pole became archbishop of Canterbury.

Richard Chancellor, instigator of the Muscovy Company, died in a shipwreck.

1557

Death of Anne of Cleves, fourth wife of Henry VIII.

War declared between England and France to support Spain.

First bond of the Lords of the Congregation, organization of Scottish
  Protestantism.

1558

English expelled from Calais, last ofthe French possessions (7
  January).

Mary Queen of Scots married the French dauphin, Francis.

Death of Mary I (Mary Tudor) (17 November). Her half-sister
  became queen of England as Elizabeth I.

Death of Cardinal Pole.

1559

Colloquy of Westminster.

Treaty of Cateau-Cambresis: a European settlement between the
  Empire, France, and England.

Third Act of Uniformity and Act of Supremacy in England, signed by
  Elizabeth, settled the question of religion. Elizabeth became head of
  the English Church.

Mary Queen of Scots became queen of France on the accession of her
  husband.

John Knox returned to Scotland where he introduced Presbyterianism.

Elizabethan Book of Common Prayer published (revised 1662).

Completion by John Foxe of *Foxe's Book of Martyrs* (begun 1554).

Matthew Parker became archbishop of Canterbury (until 1575).

1560

Treaty of Berwick (27 February): the Scottish protestant Lords of the
  Congregation were promised English aid against the French.

Elizabeth sent Lord Grey with an army to help the Scottish Lords of
  the Congregation.

Death of Mary of Guise, the Scottish regent.

Mary Queen of Scots widowed by the death of Francis II of France.

The Treaty of Edinburgh, enacting peace between England and
  Scotland, signed: French forces to quit Scotland.

Scottish Parliament abolished Roman Catholicism in Scotland.

Establishment of the Reformed Church of Scotland.

First Book of Discipline in Scottish Church.

Death in a fall of Amy Robsart, wife of Robert Dudley, later Earl of
  Leicester.
Sussex became Lord Lieutenant of Ireland (until 1564).

1561

Mary Queen of Scots landed in Scotland.

1562

Treaty of Hampton Court between Elizabeth and the Prince de Condé
  (signed 21 September).
English force landed to help the Huguenots in France: Havre
  occupied.
Battle of Corrichie: rebel troops under Earl of Huntly defeated by
  Mary's troops under Moray, half-brother of Mary; Huntly killed.

1563

Havre evacuated by the English.
Agreement by Convocation of the Church of England of the Thirty-
  nine Articles.
Plague in London.

1564

Mary Queen of Scots married Lord Darnley (29 July); Moray fled to
  England.
First punishments of Puritans in England.

1566

Birth of a son (later James VI of Scotland and James I of England)
  born to Mary Queen of Scots and Lord Darnley (19 June).
Murder of Rizzio, secretary of Mary Queen of Scots.
First organized Lord Mayor's Show in London.

1567

Murder of Lord Darnley (10 February) near Edinburgh. Mary Queen
  of Scots married Bothwell.
Mary Queen of Scots taken prisoner by Scottish nobles at the
  bloodless Battle of Carberry Hill, imprisoned in Lochleven Castle,
  and compelled to abdicate.
Scottish Parliament declared Mary guilty of murder and to have
  forfeited the crown: the infant James VI proclaimed king of
  Scotland. Moray became regent.
Shane O'Neill defeated and killed in Ireland.

1568

Mary escaped from Lochleven: defeated by Moray at the Battle of
Langside (13 May); fled to England. Imprisoned by Elizabeth I.

1569

Spanish treasure ships seized at Falmouth and Southampton.
Beggars of the Sea first appeared.

1570

Assassination of Regent Moray; Lennox became regent of Scotland.
Elizabeth I declared deposed by Pope Pius V in the second Bull of
Deposition.
Incorporation of Oxford University by Elizabeth I.

1571

Thirty-nine Articles enacted by Parliament.
Beginning of penal legislation against Catholics in England.
Regent Lennox murdered in Scotland: Earl of Mar became regent.
Foundation of Jesus College, Oxford, by Hugh Price.
Opening of the Royal Exchange, founded by Sir Thomas Gresham.

1572

Defensive alliance between France and England.
Execution of the rebel Earl of Northumberland by beheading.
Death of Regent Mar in Scotland: Morton succeeded.
Death of John Knox (24 November).

1573

Pacification of Perth. Edinburgh Castle surrendered by Kirkcaldy of
Grange and Maitland of Lethington.

1576

Opening of the first permanent English theatre, in London.

1577

Drake's voyage round the world in the *Golden Hind* began (13
December, completed 1580).
Discovery of the siphon principle by William Welwood.

1578

Morton resigned the regency of Scotland, but afterwards took
possession of the king.
Publication of Holinshed's *Chronicles*.

1579

Publication of Spenser's *The Shepherd 's Calendar* and Lyly's *Euphues*.

1580

Colonization of Ireland. Battle of Glen Malone: Irish clans defeated English settlers.

Francis Drake completed first English circumnavigation of the world (26 September).

c.1580

Congregational Movement founded by Robert Browne.

1581

Morton put to death in Scotland.

Edmund Campion, Jesuit missionary to England, hanged (beatified 1886).

Second Book of Discipline in Scotland.

Francis Drake knighted by Elizabeth I on his ship, the *Golden Hind* (4 April).

The English trading venture, the Levant Company, founded.

1582

Raid of Ruthven (22 August): James VI of Scotland a prisoner of the English in Ruthven Castle (until June 1583).

Death of George Buchanan, Scottish scholar and historian, and tutor of James VI.

Marriage of William Shakespeare and Anne Hathaway (27 November).

Edinburgh University founded.

1583

Newfoundland annexed by Britain: Sir Humphrey Gilbert's voyage to found a colony there. During the voyage home his ship sank off the Azores and all perished (9 September).

Whitgift became archbishop of Canterbury to suppress Puritanism.

Execution of the rebel Earl of Desmond.

Edward Arden, English High Sheriff, hanged.

Cambridge University Press founded by Thomas Thomas.

1584

Association formed to protect Elizabeth.

Episcopacy established in Scottish Church by James VI.

Sir John Perrot became Lord Deputy of Ireland (until 1588).

Execution by beheading of Lord Ruthven, one of the conspirators in the Raid of Ruthven.

1585

Drake commissioned for reprisals in West Indies. Caragena in
  Colombia captured by him.

North Carolina first settled (permanently 1663).

English Act against Jesuits, seminary priests, etc.

Earl of Leicester landed in Holland with a force to support the Dutch
  (December).

Babington Plot to murder Elizabeth I devised by Anthony Babington.

Suppression of provincial printing offices by order of the Star
  Chamber (23 June).

Foundation of Oxford University Press.

1586

Leicester made Governor-General of United Provinces.

Death of Sir Philip Sidney from wounds sustained in an attack on
  Spanish convoy at Zutphen in the Netherlands (September).

Babington Plot exposed by Walsingham (August): Babington
  executed.

Trial of Mary Queen of Scots for treason (14–15 October).

Alliance between Elizabeth and James VI for defence of Protestantism.

1587

Execution of Mary Queen of Scots by beheading at Fotheringhay
  Castle (8 February).

Anglo-Spanish War. Drake's expediton to Cadiz where he destroyed
  over 100 Spanish vessels to delay sailing of Spanish Armada (19
  April).

Leicester left Holland (August).

Sir Walter Raleigh's second expedition to the New World landed in
  North Carolina (11 August); first child born in the New World of
  English parents, Virginia Dare (18 August).

Davis Strait, Greenland, discovered by John Davis.

Introduction of potatoes into England.

1588

Anglo-Spanish War. Spanish Armada set sail from Lisbon (20 May);
  defeated on 29 July; Armada forced to return to Spain by sailing
  north round Scotland.

'Martin Marprelate' Puritan tracts began (ended 1589): attacks on
  bishops.

The Gambia sold to English merchants by the Portuguese.

Death of the Earl of Leicester.

Invention of shorthand by Dr Timothy Bright.

1589

Failure of Drake's expedition against Portugal.

1590

Catholic reform completed (commenced *c.*1522).

1591

Anglo-Spanish War. Battle of the Azores (August): Spanish fleet defeated English fleet.

1592

Presbyterianism fully established in Scotland.

1593

Anti-Puritan Statute in England: many fled to Holland.

English Acts against Popish recusants.

Death of Christopher Marlowe in a tavern brawl (30 May).

Marischal College, Aberdeen, founded by George Keith, 5th Earl Marischal.

British statute mile established by law.

1594

First performance of Shakespeare's *Comedy of Errors* and *Titus Andronicus:* earliest of his plays.

Huntly's Rebellion. Battle of Glenlivet (4 October): rebels defeated royal troops of James VI.

1596

Triple Alliance between England, France, and United Provinces.

English expedition to Cadiz: Cadiz captured.

Sir Robert Cecil became Secretary of State.

The Lambeth Articles concerning predestination and election drawn up by John Whitgift, archbishop of Canterbury.

Publication of Spenser's *Faerie Queene.*

Foundation of Sidney Sussex College, Cambridge, by the terms of the will of Lady Frances Sidney, Countess Dowager of Sussex.

Invention of the water closet by Sir John Harington.

Death of Sir Francis Drake (28 January).

1597

Publication of *The Ecclesiastical Polity* of Richard Hooker.

1599

Earl of Essex became Lord Deputy of Ireland: disgraced on his
  return.

1600

Birth of a son (later Charles I) to James VI of Scotland and Anne of
  Denmark (19 November).
Gowrie Conspiracy in Scotland.
East India Company founded in England (dissolved 1858).
Dr William Gilbert published *De Magnete,* his pioneer work describ-
  ing the magnetism of the Earth.

1601

Rebellion and execution of the Earl of ssex.
Great English Poor Law Act passed.
O'Neill's Rebellion. Kinsale taken by Spanish troops supporting
  rebels (September). Royal troops besieged Kinsale and defeated
  Spaniards and Irish rebels at Battle of Kinsale (24 December).
First use of fruit juice as a preventative of scurvy by James Lancaster.

1602

First performance of Shakespeare's *Hamlet.*
Opening of the Bodleian Library founded (1598) by Sir Thomas Bodley.

1603

Death of Elizabeth I (24 March). James VI of Scotland became king
  of England as James I of England: Union of the Crowns.
Earl of Tyrone submitted: Ireland conquered.
Translation of Montaigne's *Essays* into English by John Florio.

1604

Hampton Court Conference of clergy failed to reach agreement
  between Puritans and High Churchmen.
Revision of the Thirty-nine Articles.
Peace between England, Spain and the Netherlands.
Scottish Civil Wars. Battle of Glen Fruin: Highlanders defeated royal
  force under Duke of Argyll.

1605

The Gunpowder Plot to blow up the Houses of Parliament discovered
  (5 November).

1606

Adoption of the Union Jack as the flag of England (12 April).

Execution by hanging of Guy Fawkes, one of the instigators of the
  Gunpowder Plot (31 January).
The London Company chartered to colonize in Virginia.

1607

Proposals to unite Scotland and England rejected by English Parliament.
Battle of Gibraltar: Heemskerk annihilated Spanish fleet.
Earls of Tyrone and Tyrconnel left Ireland for ever with their families.
London Company colonized Virginia. Establishment of the first
  permanent English settlement at Jamestown (13 May).
Appearance of Halley's Comet (named after Edmund Halley).

1609

English Baptist Church formed at Amsterdam (and 1611 in London).
Bermuda settled by British (formally taken over 1684).

1610

James VI and I dissolved his first Parliament: constitutional struggle
  began.
Plantation of Ulster began.
Publication of the Douai Bible, first English Catholic translation of
  the Bible, complete (began 1609).
Hudson's Bay discovered by Henry Hudson.

1611

The Authorized Version of the Bible published.
James VI and I created the title of baronet.

1612

James VI and I established Episcopacy in Scotland.
English factory founded at Surat in India.
Wadham College, Oxford, founded by bequest of Nicholas Wadham.

1613

Marriage in Virginia of Pocahontas, daughter of an American Indian
  chief, and John Rolfe.

1614

Addled Parliament in England sat (5 April), dissolved by James I (7
  June); it passed no bills..
Napier of Merchiston introduced logarithms.

1615

Sir Thomas Roe became resident English ambassador at court of
  Great Mogul in India.

Death in prison of Arabella Stewart, heir to the English throne.
Circulation of blood discovered by William Harvey.

1616

Death of William Shakespeare (23 April).
Fall of Somerset, favourite of James VI and I: Buckingham in power.
Baffin Bay discovered by William Baffin (*c*.1584–1622).
Ben Jonson became first poet laureate.
John Rolfe and Pocahontas came to England.

1617

Henry Briggs introduced the decimal notation.
Death of John Napier (4 April).

1618

The Five Articles of Perth accepted by a pseudo General Assembly.
Sir Walter Raleigh executed for treason by beheading (29 October).
Epsom salts discovered.

1619

Slavery introduced in Virginia.

1620

The Pilgrim Fathers set sail in the *Mayflower* for New England (6
    September, arrived 21 December/16 December OS).
Massachusetts first settled.
The *Novum Organum* of Francis Bacon.
Manufacture of coke patented by Dud Dudley.

c.1620

Epsom races first run.

1621

English Parliament attacked monopolies; dissolved after Protestation
    of its Rights.
Five Articles of Perth passed by Scottish Parliament.
Fall of Francis Bacon.

1622

First English newspaper appeared.

1623

Death of William Jaggard, publisher of Shakespeare's works.
Abolition of the right of sanctuary for criminals in England.
Death of Anne Hathaway, widow of William Shakespeare.

1624

Monopoly Act in England: patents protected.

Foundation of Pembroke College, Oxford (as Broadgates Hall).

1625

Death of James VI and I (27 March). His son became became king of England, Scotland and Ireland as Charles I.

Parliament gave Charles I tonnage and poundage for one year only.

Treaty of Southampton: between England and the United Provinces.

Failure of English expedition to Cadiz.

Triple Alliance between England, Denmark and Holland.

Barbados formally occupied by the English.

Post of Master of the King's Musick originated. Nicholas Lanier first Master.

*c.***1625**

The size of bricks standardized in England.

1627

English Treaty with Huguenots.

Impeachment of Buckingham.

Forced loan in England; Sir John Eliot and others imprisoned.

English settlement of Barbados.

Death of Francis Bacon, Lord Verulam (9 April).

1627

Anglo-French Wars. St Martin, capital of Ile de Ré in the Bay of Biscay unsuccessfully besiged by the Duke of Buckingham (17 July–29 October); retreating English troops suffered bad losses.

1628

Petition of Right, protecting the 'rights and liberties of the subject', passed by Parliament and received Royal Assent of Charles I.

Murder of Buckingham, favourite of James VI and I, by John Felton (23 August): Felton hanged.

Harvey published *De Motu Cordis*, revealing his discovery of the circulation of the blood.

Massachusetts Bay Company granted territory.

1629

Charles I dissolved his third Parliament and began eleven years of arbitrary government.

Peace between England and France.

1630

Birth of a son (later Charles II) to King Charles I and Henrietta Maria of France (29 May).

Treaty of Madrid between England and Spain.

Settlement of Surinam (Netherlands Guiana) by the English.

1631

Death of the poet John Donne.

New Hampshire founded by John Mason.

1632

Death in prison of the parliamentarian Sir John Eliot.

1633

Birth of a second son (later James II) to Charles I and Henrietta Maria.

Sir Thomas Wentworth, 1st Earl of Strafford, became Lord Deputy of Ireland.

William Laud became archbishop of Canterbury (until 1645).

Death of George Herbert.

1634

Ship money began to be demanded by Charles I without the consent of Parliament.

Maryland settled.

1635

Connecticut first settled.

c.1635

Invention of the flintlock.

1636

John Hampden refused to pay ship money (and 1637).

Hackney carriages in use by now in London.

First settlement of Rhode Island.

1637

Laud's *Liturgy* published in Scotland: popular indignation.

John Hampden condemned by the judges.

Death of the poet and playwright Ben Jonson (6 August).

1638

Establishment of Presbyterianism in Scotland again. The National Covenant signed in Scotland. The Glasgow Assembly met.

British Honduras (now Belize) settled by the English.

1639

First Bishops' War: ended by Peace of Berwick between England and Scotland.

Act of Toleration in England established religious toleration.

1640

The Short Parliament in England (April-May).

Second Bishops' War began: ended by Treaty of Ripon: a Parliament to be called.

Long Parliament met (November): purged 1648, expelled 1653, recalled 1659, dissolved 1660.

Impeachment of Laud.

1641

Execution of Strafford.

Charles I set out for Scotland.

Irish Rebellion. Drogheda besieged (December) by rebels under Owen Roe O'Neill.

Abolition by the Long Parliament of the Star Chamber, English court of prerogative inaugurated in the 14th century.

Grand Remonstrance indictment of Charles I voted and published by English Parliament (November).

Death of the Flemish-born court painter Sir Anthony van Dyck (9 December).

1642

Attempt to seize the Five Members of the Commons.

English Civil War. Outbreak when Charles I raised his standard at Nottingham (22 August); Battle of Edgehill between Charles I and the Parliamentary forces (23 October): victory claimed by both sides.

Irish Rebellion: O'Neill ended siege of English garrison at Drogheda (March).

General Assembly of Confederated Catholics in Kilkenny.

The English religious movement Fifth Monarchy Men active (until 1661).

English theatres closed by the Puritans (until 1660).

Tasman's voyage: discovery of Van Dieman's Land (now Tasmania) (24 November; rediscovery of New Zealand (13 December).

1643

English Parliament abolished Episcopacy.

Westminster Assembly began its sessions (until 1649).

English Civil War. Battle of Stratton (16 May): Royalist victory over
Parliamentary troops; Battle of Chalgrove Field, Oxfordshire (18
June): between the Royalists and the Parliamentarians; John
Hampden killed; Battle of Adwalton Moor or Atherton Moor (30
June): Parliamentary forces under the Fairfaxes defeated; Battle of
Lansdowne (5 July): Royalist victory over Parliamentarians under
Waller; Battle of Roundway Down (13 July): Sir William Waller's
Parliamentary army destroyed; Royalists under Prince Rupert
stormed Bristol; Battle of Newbury (20 September): drawn:
Falkland killed. Battle of Winceby: victory of Sir Thomas Fairfax
and Oliver Cromwell.

Battle of Ross: Irish rebels defeated by Ormonde.

Solemn League and Covenant: agreement between English Parliament and the Scots.

First English medal struck by Charles I.

Rediscovery of Tonga by Tasman.

Death of John Pym, Parliamentary leader.

1644

English Civil War. Battle of Alresford (29 March): Parliamentarians
under Sir William Waller defeated the Royalists with heavy losses;
Battle of Selby (11 April): Royalists defeated by Parliamentarians
under Sir Thomas Fairfax; Battle of Copredy Bridge (29 June):
defeat of Waller; Battle of Marston Moor (2 July): Parliamentary
victory over Royalists due to Cromwell, aided by Scots; Battle of
Tippermuir (1 September): Scottish Royalists under Montrose
victorious over Covenanters; Capitulation of Parliamentary army
under Essex at Battle of Lostwithiel (2 September); Battle of
Aberdeen (13 September): Covenanters defeated by Royalist troops
under Montrose; Second Battle of Newbury (27 October): Parliamentary success.

Scots entered England under Alexander Leslie, Earl of Leven.

Parliament captured York.

1645

Execution of Archbishop Laud by beheading (10 January).

Uxbridge negotiations between Charles I and Parliament.

New Model Army organized under Sir Thomas Fairfax.

English Civil War. Battle of Inverlochy (2 February): Montrose's victory over Covenanters and Campbells; Battle of Auldearn (9 May): Montrose's victory over Covenanters; Battle of Naseby between Parliamentarians and Royalists (14 June): victory of Fairfax and Cromwell over Charles I and Rupert; Battle of Alford (2 July): Montrose's Royalist victory over the Covenanters; Battle of Langport (10 July): Parliamentarian victory under Fairfax; Battle of Kilsyth (15 August): Montrose's victory over Covenanters; Battle of Philiphaugh (13 September): Montrose defeated by Covenanters under David Leslie; Battle of Rowton Heath (24 September): Parliamentary defeat of Royalist cavalry.

Self-denying Ordinance.

Royalists sacked Leicester.

Fairfax took Bristol.

Execution of the Jesuit missionary in England, Henry Morse.

1646

Fairfax took Exeter and Oxford.

Charles I surrendered to the Scottish army.

1647

Charles I handed over to English Parliament.

Cornet Joyce carried off Charles I.

'Heads of the Proposals' prepared by Ireton.

Army marched on London.

'The Agreement of the People' prepared by the English republican and democratic group, the Levellers.

Charles I escaped to Carisbrooke Castle.

'The Engagement' between Charles I and the Scots.

Irish Rebellion. Battle of Dunganhill (8 August): Irish rebels defeated by English.

Foundation of the Quakers (Society of Friends) by George Fox.

1648

Commons passed 'Vote of No Addresses'.

English Civil War. Battle of Preston (17–19 August): Cromwell defeated the Scots under Hamilton.

Fairfax took Colchester.

Failure of Newport negotiations between Parliament and Charles I.

Charles I declined terms offered by the army.

Pride's Purge of the Long Parliament (6 December) by General
   Thomas Pride: remnant named Rump Parliament.
The Diggers group of English communists active between now and
   1652: among them Gerrard Winstanley.
Publication of *Hesperides* by Robert Herrick.

1649

Execution of Charles I (30 January). Commonwealth republican
   regime in England (until 1653).
English Parliament abolished the House of Lords and the monarchy.
The Levellers were crushed by Cromwell.
Charles II proclaimed king of Scotland.
Irish Campaign. Battle of Rathmines (2 August): Roundhead troops in
   Dublin defeated Royalists under the Marquis of Ormonde;
   Cromwell besieged and sacked Drogheda (12 September) and
   captured Wexford.

1650

Birth of a son (later William III) posthumously to William II of
   Orange (4 November).
English Civil War. Battle of Carbisdale (27 April): Orkney Royalists
   and Swedish mercenaries under Montrose defeated by Parliamentar-
   ians; Montrose captured by David Leslie and executed by hanging
   (21 May).
Agreement of Breda between Charles II and the Scots.
Cromwell left Ireland, leaving Ireton in command.
Scottish Campaign. Battle of Dunbar (3 September): English under
   Cromwell defeated the Scots under Leslie.

c.1650

Coffee brought to England.

1651

English Civil War. Charles II crowned at Scone (January). Battle of
   Worcester (3 September): Scottish Royalists under Charles II
   defeated by Parliamentarians under Cromwell; Charles fled to
   France.
Navigation Act passed by English Parliament.
Publication of *The Leviathan* by Thomas Hobbes.
Foundation of the religious sect of Muggletonians by the tailors
   Lodowicke Muggleton and John Reeve.

1652

Monck subdued Scotland.

Act for Settling of Ireland.

Anglo-Dutch Wars. Battle of Dover (29 November): Van Tromp
  defeated Blake off Dungeness.

Bengal became an English settlement about now.

1653

Anglo-Dutch Wars. Battle of Portland (18–20 February): Dutch under
  Van Tromp defeated by Blake; Battle of Leghorn (31 March): naval
  victory of Dutch fleet over English; Battle of Texel (2–3 June):
  British fleet defeated Dutch.

Rump Parliament (residue of Long Parliament) dissolved by
  Cromwell (20 April).

Barebone's Parliament met, 4 July to 12 December (named after
  Praise-God Barebone, one of its members.

Cromwell accepted the Instrument of Government and became
  Protector (16 December).

Publication of *The Compleat Angler* by Izaak Walton.

1654

Peace between England and Holland.

General Monck made governor of Scotland (until 1660) by
  Cromwell.

1655

Treaty of Westminster between France and England.

Anglo-Spanish War began with capture of Jamaica from Spain by the
  British (May).

1656

Cromwell accepted the Humble Petition and Advice, and assumed the
  title of Lord Protector after refusing that of King.

Act of Union between Scotland and England (annulled at Restoration).

Death of Cromwell from pneumonia (3 September): Richard
  Cromwell Lord Protector (until 1659).

Anglo-Spanish War. Blake captured the Plate fleet. Blake destroyed
  Spanish fleet at Teneriffe.

Treaty of Paris between England and France.

Foundation of the Grenadier Guards (30 May).

First recorded mention of tea in Britain.

1659

Rump Parliament (Long Parliament) reassembled.

Abdication of Richard Cromwell.

Concert of the Hague: Holland, France and England against Sweden.

Coldstream Guards raised.

Cheques first used, the date on the first known to have been drawn
being 6 February.

1660

Monck arrived in London and demanded a dissolution of Parliament;
Long Parliament dissolved, and a new Parliament, the Cavalier
Parliament, met (until 1678).

Fourth Act of Uniformity.

General Letter Office established by Act of Parliament.

Clarendon became chief minister (until 1667).

Restoration of Charles II (29 May—Oak Apple Day) Reopening of
theatres in Britain.

Composition of light discovered by Newton.

Organization of the Royal Society of London (granted Royal Charter
1662).

*c.*1660

The formula of laudanum developed by Thomas Sydenham.

1661

Savoy Conference failed to make agreement between Puritans and
other Churchmen.

Treaty between England and Portugal: England obtained Tangier and
Bombay as a marriage dowry.

Episcopacy established in Scotland by decree.

Corporation Act: first of a series of Acts against Puritans.

Board of Trade founded in London (now Department of Trade and
Industry and incorporating since 1992 the Department of Energy).

Island of St Helena appropriated by the British East India Company.

Hand-struck postage stamps first used.

*c.*1661

Opening of Vauxhall Gardens in London (closed 1859).

1662

Birth of a daughter (later Mary II) to James, Duke of York (later
James II) and Anne Hyde.

Press Act in England.
Act of Uniformity in England: led to ejection of many clergy:
  beginning of English Nonconformity.
Patronage restored by Scottish Parliament.
Royal Society incorporated (22 April).
Treaty between England and Holland.
Act for the Settlement of Ireland.
Dunkirk sold to France by Charles II.

1663

Battle of Amegial: Spaniards under Don Juan defeated Portuguese
  and their English allies.
First Drury Lane Theatre in London opened.

1664

First Conventicle Act in England.
English expedition seized New Netherland and changed New
  Amsterdam to New York, after James Duke of York (8 September);
  Richard Nicolls became first governor of New York (until 1667).
Formation of the Royal Marine Corps (as the Duke of York and
  Albany's Maritime Regiment of Foot).

1665

Birth of a second daughter (later Queen Anne) to the Duke of York
  (later James II) and Anne Hyde (6 February).
Battle of Lowestoft (3 June) between English and Dutch fleets:
  English victory over Dutch.
Buccaneers' Raids. Porto Bello sacked by Henry Morgan.
Great Plague in London.
Five Mile Act.

1666

Louis XIV declared war against England.
Anglo-Dutch Wars. Battle of the Downs (1–3 June): battle between
  English and Dutch fleets; Battle of the Goodwins (1–4 July): defeat
  of British fleet in Four Days' Naval Battle; Battle of North Foreland
  (4 August): Dutch fleet defeated by English.
Great Fire in London (2-6 September): Fleet Prison burned down.
Fire insurance pioneered by Nicholas Barbon, son of Praise-God
  Barebone.
The use of semaphore signalling pioneered by Lord Worcester.

Covenanters' Rising. Battle of Rullion Green (November): Scottish
  Covenanters defeated by royal troops.
Discovery of the spectrum of sunlight by Newton.

1667

Act of English Parliament against Irish cattle trade.
Anglo-Dutch Wars. Battle of St Kitts (10 May): British victory over
  French and Dutch fleets; Battle of Sheerness (7 June): Dutch fleet in
  the Thames.
Peace of Breda between England and the United Netherlands.
Surinam (Netherlands Guiana) ceded by England to the Netherlands.
Fall of Clarendon in England.
Publication of *Paradise Lost* by John Milton.
Boyle's Law discovered by Robert Boyle.
Fire plugs first put into water mains.

1668

Cabal ministry formed (ended 1673) by Charles II: the name comes
  from the names of members: Clifford, Ashley (Shaftesbury),
  Buckingham, Arlington, Lauderdale.
Triple Alliance: England, Holland and Sweden.
Dryden became the first poet laureate (13 April, resigned 1689).

1669

Ormonde recalled from Ireland: restored in 1667.
The Sheldonian Theatre built at Oxford by Gilbert Sheldon, archbishop of Canterbury.

1670

Second Conventicle Act.
Secret Treaty of Dover between Charles II and Louis XIV to re-
  establish Catholicism in England: also a sham public treaty.
Hudson's Bay Company chartered by Charles II.
South Carolina and Wisconsin settled permanently.

1671

Buccaneers' Raids. Henry Morgan attacked Panama City (18
  January) and plundered it; withdrew with plunder and prisoners (24
  February).
Attempt to steal the crown jewels from the Tower of London by
  Colonel Thomas Blood (9 May).
Death of Anne Hyde, wife of James, Duke of York (later James II).

1672

Stop of the Exchequer in England.

First Declaration of Indulgence issued.

England declared war against Holland.

Treaty between Sweden and England.

Anglo-Dutch Wars. Battle of Southwold Bay (7 June): De Ruyter defeated an Anglo-French fleet under the Duke of York.

Footlights first used in British theatres.

Leather hose invented for fire-fighting.

1673

Test Act passed, against Catholic office-holding: Cabal ministry dissolved: Danby in power.

Charles II cancelled Declaration of Indulgence.

Anglo-Dutch Wars. Battles of Schooneveld: De Ruyter against Rupert: both drawn. Battle of Kykduin: De Ruyter defeated Anglo-French fleet.

Marriage of James, Duke of York (later James II) and Mary of Modena.

1674

Peace between England and Holland.

Pondicherry founded by French in India.

Second Drury Lane Theatre in London opened.

Death of John Milton (8 November).

1675

Shaftesbury organized an opposition in Parliament: beginning of Whig Party.

Letters of Intercommuning in Scotland against Covenanters.

Dr John Fell appointed bishop of Oxford.

Building of the Royal Observatory at Greenwich, founded by Charles II, betgan (10 August, moved to Sussex in the 1950s).

1676

Bacon's Rebellion, American revolt in Virginia led by Nathaniel Bacon.

Binomial Theorem invented before now by Newton.

1677

Marriage of William of Orange and Mary, daughter of James, Duke of York (later James II) (4 November).

1678

End of Cavalier Parliament.

Treaty between England and Holland.

Unsolved murder of the MP Sir Edmund Berry Godfrey. Invention by Titus Oates of the 'Popish Plot' to murder Charles II: cause of agitation 1678-81.

Extension of the Test Act to peers.

Beginning of the Exclusion Struggle against the succession of James, Duke of York (ended 1681).

1679

Fall of Danby.

Archbishop Sharp murdered by Scottish Covenanters.

Exclusion Bill introduced by English Parliament.

Covenanters' Rising. Battle of Drumclog (11 June): Covenanters defeated Graham of Claverhouse; Battle of Bothwell Bridge (22 June): Covenanters defeated by the English under the Duke of Monmouth.

Habeas Corpus Act became law in England (27 May): principle previously stated in Magna Carta and confirmed by Petition of Right.

Black Letter first used for English newspaper titles.

Meal Tub Plot: a fictitious plot to prevent the accession of James, conceived by Thomas Dangerfield: Dangerfield found guilty of perjury.

The Tories first so named.

c.1679

The Whigs so named.

1680

Petitioners (political group connected with the Whigs) and Abhorrers for and against Exclusion Bill: beginning of English party system.

House of Lords rejected Exclusion Bill.

Covenanters' Rising. Sanquhar Declaration: Charles II disowned by strong Covenanters. Battle of Aird's Moss: Richard Cameron killed.

Buccaneers' Raids. John Coxon defeated and captured Spanish vessels at Panama.

1681

Donald Cargill executed in Scotland.

Oil lighting first used in streets in London.

1682

Ashmolean Museum, Oxford, opened (founded *c.*1677 by Elias
  Ashmole.
Advocates' Library, Edinburgh (now National Library of Scotland)
  founded.
Thomas Dongan, Earl of Limerick, made governor of New York.
Appearance of Halley's Comet (named after Edmund Halley).
Foundation of Pennsylvania by the English Quaker William Penn.

1683

Birth of a son in Germany (later George II) to George (later Elector of
  Hanover and George I) (10 November).
City of London charter forfeited.
Rye House Plot by Whigs to assassinate Charles II discovered.
Execution of Algernon Sidney and Lord Russell for alleged involve-
  ment in the Rye House Plot.
Opening of the Ashmolean Museum, Oxford, the first museum in
  Britain (6 June).
Death of Izaak Walton (15 December).

1684

Publication of *Pilgrim's Progress* by John Bunyan.
The Law of Gravity established by Isaac Newton.

1685

Death of Charles II from apoplexy (6 February). His brother became
  king as James VII of Scotland and II of England.
Duke of Monmouth, illegitimate son of Charles II and Lucy Walter,
  proclaimed himself king and led Monmouth's Rebellion (11 June to
  6 July); Battle of Sedgmoor (6 July) between James II and the Duke
  of Monmouth: defeat of Monmouth; Execution of Monmouth by
  beheading (15 July).
  Jeffreys and the Bloody Assizes: 320 rebels executed, including the
  Earl of Argyll, and 800 transported.

1686

James II disregarded the Test Act and appointed Catholics to public
  office.
Tyrconnel commander-in-chief in Ireland.

1687

Tyrconnel became viceroy of Ireland.

Second Declaration of Indulgence.

Buccaneers' Raids. Naval encounter between buccaneering ships and
   Spanish ships (27 April–3 May).

Invention of the repeating watch by Daniel Quare.

Revival of the Order of the Thistle.

Death of Nell Gwyn, mistress of Charles II (13 November).

1688

Birth of a son (later James Stewart, the 'Old Pretender') to James II
   and Mary of Modena, his second wife (10 June).

Execution of James Renwick, last Covenanting martyr.

Seven Bishops put on trial for sedition under the terms of the
   Declaration of Indulgence were acquitted.

Invitation to William of Orange and Mary to ascend the throne.

William of Orange landed in England (November); flight of James II
   to France.

Outbreak of the War of the Grand Alliance (ended 1697) between
   France and the Allies (Austria, the Netherlands, England, Spain and
   certain German states): in England called King William's War.

First allusion to Lloyd's of London (as Edward Lloyd's Coffee
   House) (February).

Death of John Bunyan (31 August).

1689

House of Commons declared the English throne vacant: William and
   Mary declared joint sovereigns (13 February) and crowned (11 April).

Scottish Parliament declared that James had forfeited the Scottish
   crown: William and Mary chosen.

Toleration Act granted freedom of worship to Protestant dissenters.

Declaration of Rights in England (February). Bill of Rights, based on
   Declaration of Rights, passed by Parliament in England (October).
   Royal powers limited.

War of the English Succession. Siege of Londonderry by James II
   began (19 April), ultimately relieved (30 July); Battle of Newtown
   Butler (31 July): James's army defeated: Sligo fell, but recovered by
   Sarsfield.

Jacobite Rebellion. Battle of Killiecrankie (27 July): Jacobites
   defeated royal force, Claverhouse killed in hour of victory; Battle of
   Dunkeld (21 August): rebel attack defeated.

First Battle of Bantry Bay: French attempted the invasion of Ireland.
Members of the British clergy who refused to take the oath of
   allegiance called Nonjurors (until 1805).
Abolition of poll tax.
First perforfmance of the opera *Dido and Aeneas* by Henry Purcell.
Death of Judge Jeffreys in the Tower of London (18 April).

1690

Jacobite Rebellion. Battle of Cromdale: rebels finally overcome.
War of the English Succession. Battle of Beachy Head (30 June–10
   July): French naval victory by Tourville over England and Holland;
   Battle of the Boyne in Ireland (1 July) between William III and
   James II: James defeated and fled to France: commander in chief of
   British forces in Ireland, Schomberg, killed.
First Siege of Limerick (soon raised).
Scottish Parliament abolished the Lords of the Articles and lay
   patronage and re-established Presbyterianism finally: Scottish
   Parliament became a real power in Scotland.
Publication of *Essay Concerning Human Understanding* by John Locke.

1691

War of the English Succession. Battle of Aughrim (12 July): William
   III's troops defeated Irish and French troops supporting James II.
   Galway surrendered to William's forces. Second Siege of Limerick:
   capitulated (October); Treaty of Limerick (October): freedom of
   worship for Catholics.
John Tillotson became archbishop of Canterbury (until 1694).
Death of George Fox, founder of the Society of Friends (13 January).

1692

Massacre of Glencoe (13 February): Government troops massacred
   families of the Clan MacDonald whose leader, MacIan, had been
   late taking an oath of loyalty to William III.
War of the Revolution/English Succession. Battle of La Hogue (19–
   20 May): Russell's naval victory over French; Battle of Steenkerke
   or Steinkirk (3 August): unsuccessful attack by the English under
   William III on the French.
Nathum Tate became poet laureate.

1693

Dutch took Pondicherry.

War of the English Succession. Battle of Lagos (17 June): French
  naval attack on Dutch and English fleet under Sir George Rooke;
  Battle of Neerwinden (29 July): English under William III defeated
  by French.
The 'Alfred Jewel' found at Athelney (now in the Ashmolean
  Museum, Oxford).
The Cabinet form of government formally instituted by William III
  and its principles developed by Sir Robert Walpole.

1694

National Debt came into effect in England.
Bank of England founded by William Paterson.
Triennal Act.
Death of Queen Mary from smallpox (28 December); William III
  became sole sovereign.
Introduction of stamp duty in England.
Opening of the Royal Hospital, Chelsea (designed by Christopher
  Wren).
Thomas Tenison became archbishop of Canterbury.

1695

William III took Namur.
Freedom of Press established in England.
Darien Scheme proposed by William Paterson.
Anti-Catholic legislation in Ireland.
Bank of Scotland founded by the Scottish Parliament (1 November).
Death of the composer Henry Purcell (21 November).

1696

Recoinage Act.
Assassination Plot against William III detected.
First settlement at Princeton, New Jersey.

1697

Irish Parliament refused full ratification of the Articles of Limerick.
Treaty of of Ryswick (September) ends the War of the Grand Alliance
  between France and the Allies.
Official opening of St Paul's Cathedral (2 December).
First public concert hall in London opened (Hickford's Room,
  Haymarket).

1698

First Treaty of Partition (of Spanish dominions) between Louis XIV and William III.

New East India Company founded in England.

Darien Scheme expedition to found a Scottish colony set out for Panama.

Publication of Collier's *Short View of the Immorality and Profaneness of the English Stage*.

Foundation of the Society for Promoting Christian Knowledge (SPCK) by Dr Thomas Bray.

Invention of the steam engine by Captain Thomas Savery.

1699

Second Partition Treaty.

English legislation against Irish woollen industry.

Treaty of Carlowitz between the Turks and the Allies signed.

1700

Act of Resumption in Ireland.

War of the Spanish Succession. Battle of Saragossa (20 August): Spanish attack on Allied troops withstood.

First performance of *The Way of the World* by Congreve.

The first Eddystone Lighthouse completed (begun 1698, swept away 1703).

Death of Dryden (1 May).

1701

Act of Settlement in England, securing Hanoverian succession to the throne and barring Catholics from the throne.

War of the Spanish Succession. Battle of Chiari (1 September): troops under Prince Eugène defeated French and Spanish forces.

Captain Kidd hanged for piracy (23 May).

Death of James VII in France (17 September). Louis XIV recognized his son as James III of England.

1702

Death of William III after falling from a horse (8 March). His sister-in-law succeeded as Queen Anne.

War of the Spanish Succession. Battle of Vigo Bay (12 October): British and Dutch fleet under Rooke destroyed Franco-Spanish fleet; Marlborough took Liege; failure of English attack on Cadiz.

First English daily newspaper founded (11 March)—*The Daily Courant* (ran until 1735).

1703

Act of Security in Scotland (Royal Assent next year).

Revival of the Order of the Thistle.

War of the Spanish Succession. Marlborough took Bonn; Battle of Hochstadt: Villars defeated Germans; Savoy joined Grand Alliance; Battle of Speyerbach: Allies defeated by Tallard.

Methuen Treaty between England and Portugal: another Methuen Treaty (commercial) later in same year, negotiated by John Methuen (27 December).

Buckingham Palace built by the Duke of Buckingham (rebuilt 1825-37).

Establishment of the ecclesiastical fund, Queen Anne's Bounty.

Death of the diarist Samuel Pepys (26 May).

1704

Alien Act in England.

War of the Spanish Succession. Battle of Donauwörth (2 July): Marlborough's victory; Gibraltar captured by British under Rooke (24 July); Battle of Malaga (24 August): drawn naval battle between Anglo-Dutch under Rooke and French under Toulouse; Battle of Blenheim between the English and the French (13 August): Marlborough and Eugène defeated Tallard and the Elector of Bavaria.

Invention of the negus hot drink of sweet wine and water by Colonel Negus.

1705

Marriage of Prince George (later George II) and Caroline of Anspach.

Harley and Bolingbroke became ministers in England.

War of the Spanish Succession. Battle of Alicante (29 June): British naval and marine forces seized Alicante; Battle of Cassano (16 August): victory of Prince Eugène over the French; Barcelona besieged (14 September) and captured by British under the Earl of Peterborough (9 October).

Building of Blenheim Palace began (completed 1722).

Invention of the steam pumping engine by Thomas Newcomen.

Death of Titus Oates (13 July).

1706

War of the Spanish Succession. Allies took Madrid (soon evacuated). Battle of Ramillies (23 May): British under Marlborough crushed French under Villeroi. Marlborough took Ostend.

1707

Last use of the veto by a British sovereign.

Treaty of Union between Scotland and England: Union of the Parliaments (1 May).

War of the Spanish Succession. Battle of Almanza (25 April): British defeated in Spain by Marshal Berwick. Battle of Stolhoffen (22 May): French victory; Battle of Toulon (17 July): naval attack by Dutch and British fleets unsuccessful.

Foundation of the Society of Antiquaries (reconstituted 1717, granted Royal Charter 1751).

First performance of *The Beaux' Stratagem* by George Farquhar.

1708

Harley and Bolingbroke out of office: ministry entirely Whig.

Union of the two British East India Companies.

War of the Spanish Succession. Battle of Oudenarde (or Audenarde) between the English and the French (ll July): Marlborough defeated Vendôme; Siege of Lille by Allied troops under Prince Eugène began (12 August); Battle of Wynandael (28 September): British convoy supplying Lille defeated French attack; Lille surrendered (25 October); Leake and Stanhope took Minorca from Spain (returned 1802) and Sardinia.

Legal protection of ambassadors in England introduced.

c.1708

Invention of the atmospheric pumping engine by Thomas Newcomen.

1709

First Copyright Act passed.

War of the Spanish Succession. Siege of Tournai by the British under the Duke of Marlborough began (8 July); surrendered (2 September); Battle of Malplaquet between the Allies and the French (11 September): hard-won victory by Marlborough and Prince Eugène.

First publication of *The Tatler* (12 April, until 1711), edited by Steele.

The process of pig iron production improved by Abraham Darby.

The second Eddystone Lighthouse completed (begun 1708, burned
down 1755).

1710

Harley and Bolingbroke again in office.
War of the Spanish Succession. Siege of Douai (25 April–26 June):
town taken from French by Prince Eugène; Battle of Almenara (10
July): Spanish defeated by Allied troops under General Stanhope;
Madrid again occupied by Allies; Battle of Brihuega (9 December):
British under the Earl of Stanhope defeated by the French.
Impeachment of Dr Sacheverell for a sermon.

1711

Marlborough dismissed.
First publication of *The Spectator*, edited by Addison and Steele (1
March).
Completion of the building of St Paul's Cathedral (begun 1675) by
Sir Christopher Wren.
Invention of the tuning fork by John Shore.
Incorporation of the South Sea Company.
Ascot Race Meeting first held (11 August).

1712

Imposition of soap tax (abolition 1853).
Peers created in British Parliament to pass peace clauses.
War of the Spanish Succession. Battle of Denain (24 July): Allied
forces under the Earl of Albemarle defeated by Villars.
Last trial for witchcraft in England (of Jane Wenham).
Lay patronage restored in Scottish Church against Scottish opinion.

1713

Second Barrier Treaty between Britain and Holland.
Signature of the Treaty of Utrecht (11 April) ended War of the
Spanish Succession: Acadia, Newfoundland, Nova Scotia, St Kitts-
Nevis ceded by France to Britain; Gibraltar and Minorca ceded by
Spain to Britain.

1714

Death of Anne (1 August): end of the Stewart succession. George I,
elector of Hanover, son of Sophia, granddaughter of James VI and I,
became king of Great Britain: beginning of the Hanoverian dynasty.

Quarrel between Harley (Earl of Oxford) and St John (Lord
  Bolingbroke): former dismissed.
Whig Ministry: Townshend, Stanhope, Walpole, etc.
Publication of *The Rape of the Lock* by Alexander Pope.

1715

Riot Act passed.
Jacobite Rebellion in Scotland and northern England, an attempt to
  restore the throne to James Edward Stewart, 'the Old Pretender',
  son of James II; Battle of Preston (13 November): Jacobites
  defeated and their army surrendered; Battle of Sheriffmuir (13
  November): indecisive battle between Jacobites and Royalists;
  James Edward landed at Peterhead (22 December).
Third Dutch Barrier Treaty.
Commercial treaty between Britain and Spain.
Doggett's Coat and Badge Prize, rowing competition on the Thames,
  founded by Thomas Doggett.

1716

Septenniel Act of Britain: general elections to be held every seven
  years.
Commercial treaty between Britain and Holland.
Treaty of Westminster between Britain and the Emperor.

1717

Bangorian controversy.
Whig Split: Stanhope became chief minister.
Triple Alliance: France, Britain, and Holland.
The Mother Grand Lodge of Freemasonry inaugurated in London.
John Law founded the Louisiana Company.
  Inauguration of the Mississippi Scheme as the 'Western Company'
  by John Law.
First Masonic Lodge opened in London (24 June).

1718

Charles VI joined Triple Alliance, making it a Quadruple Alliance.
War of the Quadruple Alliance. Battle of Cape Passero or Messina
  (31 July): British fleet under Admiral Sir George Byng defeated
  Spanish fleet.
Death of William Penn (30 July).

The pirate Edward Teach ('Blackbeard') killed off the coast of North
  Carolina (22 November).

*c.*1718
Inoculation for smallpox introduced into England by Lady Mary
  Wortley Montagu.

1719
Act passed empowering the English Parliament to pass laws for
  Ireland.

Publication of *Robinson Crusoe* by Daniel Defoe, based on the life of
  Alexander Selkirk.

Deaths: Joseph Addison (17 June); John Flamsteed, first Astronomer
  Royal (31 December).

1720
Atterbury's plot to restore the Stewarts.

Birth in Rome of a son, Charles Edward Stewart (later the 'Young
  Pretender' or 'Prince Charlie'), to James Edward Stewart, the 'Old
  Pretender' (31 December).

Richard Philips became governor of Nova Scotia (until 1749).

Failure of Law's Bank in France.

Quadruple Alliance joined by Spain, Denmark, and Poland.

Collapse of the South Sea Company: South Sea Bubble (exposed as
  fraud 1721).

1721
Walpole became prime minister (3 April, until 12 February 1742):
  office of prime minister introduced (legally recognized 1905).

1722
Bank of Scotland founded by John Holland who became first
  governor.

Last trial for witchcraft in Scotland.

Fire engines first acquired by a London insurance company.

Guy's Hospital in London founded by Thomas Guy.

The compensated pendulum invented by George Graham.

1723
Abolition of the right of sanctuary in England for civil offenders.

Death of Sir Christopher Wren (25 February); he was buried in St
  Paul's Cathedral.

1724

First settlement of Vermont.

Foundation of the Three Choirs Festival.

Jonathan Swift began publication of his *Drapier's Letters*.

1725

Order of the Bath founded by George I.

Alliance of Herrenhausen (or Hanover) between Britain, France, and Prussia.

The Black Watch, Highland regiment, formed (became Royal Highland Black Watch 1739).

Invention of the stereotype process by William Ged.

1726

Alliance of Herrenhausen joined by Sweden and Denmark.

Completion of St Martin-in-the-Fields in London (begun 1722) by James Gibbs.

Publication of *Gulliver's Travels* by Jonathan Swift.

First circulating library opened in Edinburgh.

Invention of the chronometer by John Harrison.

1727

Death of George I in Osnabrück of a stroke (10 June). His only son became king of Britain as George II (11 June).

Spain declared war against Britain.

First Indemnity Act for Nonconformists in England.

Publication of James Thomson's *Summer*.

First boxing title fight held in London (6 June).

Death of Sir Isaac Newton (20 March).

1728

Convention of the Pardo ended War between Spain and Britain.

First performance of *The Beggar's Opera* by John Gay.

1729

Treaty of Seville between Britain, France and Spain.

Foundation of Robert Gordon's College, Aberdeen (became Robert Gordon Institute of Technology, then The Robert Gordon University 1992).

Last burning to death of a woman as a punishment (legally abolished 1790).

Beginning of Methodist Revival.

Aberration of light discovered by James Bradley.

Death of Congreve.

1730

Colly Cibber appointed poet laureate.

1731

Britain and Holland guaranteed the Pragmatic Sanction.

Invention of the seed drill by Jethro Tull.

Invention of the sextant by John Hadley.

Death of Daniel Defoe (26 April).

1732

Foundation of Georgia in North America as a colony by James Oglethorpe.

Invention of pinchbeck, an alloy of copper and zinc, by Christopher Pinchbeck.

1733

Walpole compelled to withdraw his Excise Bill.

Invention of the flying shuttle by John Kay.

1734

Sir Robert Walpole was the first prime minister to live in 10 Downing Street (22 September).

Lloyd's List and Shipping Gazette founded.

Deaths: Lady Abigail Masham, favourite of Queen Anne; the Scottish outlaw Rob Roy (Robert MacGregor).

1736

Porteous Riots in Edinburgh (8 September) when soldiers were ordered by Captain John Porteous to fire into a crowd that had been watching the execution of a smuggler. Porteous was later hanged by a mob.

Military rank of field marshal introduced.

Repeal of statues against witchcraft.

1738

Birth of a son (later George III) to Frederick Louis, Prince of Wales (4 June).

Foundation of the first Methodist association (May) by John and Charles Wesley.

1739

The War of Jenkin's Ear broke out between Britain and Spain, caused
  by British breaking Spanish monpoly of South American trade.
Execution by hanging of Dick Turpin, highwayman (7 April).

1740

War of Jenkin's Ear. Unsuccessful British raid on Cartagena;
  circumnavigation of the world by Anson seeking Spanish ships; War
  of the Austrian Succession absorbed War of Jenkin's Ear (ended
  1748); Porto Bello in Panama captured from Spain by a British fleet
  (21 November).
Grenadier Guards organized permanently.
Publication completed (began 1739) of *A Treatise of Human Nature*
  by David Hume.
Publication of Samuel Richardson's *Pamela.*
Rule, Britannia composed by Thomas Arne to words by James
  Thomson.

1741

Royal Military Academy established at Woolwich (13 April).
Platinum discovered in England by William Brownrigg.
Death of the agriculturist Jethro Tull (21 February).

1742

Resignation of Robert Walpole: John Carteret, Earl Granville, in
  power.
First performance of Handel's *Messiah* in Dublin (13 April).
Opening of Ranelagh pleasure gardens in London (closed 1803).

1743

Treaty of Worms between Austria, Britain, and Sardinia.
War of the Austrian Succession. Battle of Dettingen (16 June): British
  and Allies under George II defeated French. Last time a British
  sovereign led troops in battle.
Sheffield plate invented.

1744

Pelham ministry in Britain.
War of the Austrian Succession. Battle of Toulon (21 February):
  British fleet under Admiral Mathews defeated by French-Spanish
  fleet; Britain captured Louisburg from America.

War declared between Britain and France.
Foundation of Sotheby's auction rooms.
First General Conference of the Methodists.
Death of Alexander Pope (30 May).

1745

Jacobite Rebellion. Prince Charles Edward Stewart landed in
  Scotland and raised his father's standard at Glenfinnan (19 August);
  Battle of Prestonpans or Gladsmuir between the Jacobites and
  government forces (21 September): Prince Charles Edward
  victorious over English royal forces under Sir John Cope; Siege of
  Carlisle begun (9 November) by Jacobites under Prince Charles
  Edward; city surrendered (14 November).
Jacobite glass manufactured (until 1765).
War of the Austrian Succession. Battle of Fontenoy between the
  French and British (11 May): defeat of British by Marshal Saxe;
  Outbreak of King George's War between Britain and France in
  North America (ended 1754); British took Cape Breton.
First medal given to all ranks: King George II's medal (also in 1746).
First performance of the national anthem, 'God Save the King', at the
  Drury Lane Theatre (28 September).
First recorded women's cricket match held in Surrey (25 July).
Death of Sir Robert Walpole, Earl of Orford (18 March).

1746

Jacobite Rebellion. Battle of Falkirk between the Young Pretender
  and General Hawley (17 January): Prince Charles victorious; Battle
  of Culloden or Drummossie Moor (16 April): Jacobites under Prince
  Charles finally crushed by the Duke of Cumberland (last battle
  fought in Britain); Prince Charles escaped to France, aided by Flora
  Macdonald and others (20 September).
War of the Austrian Succession. France captured Madras (25
  September).
Foundation of the Surgeons' Company.
Manufacture of Bow porcelain began (ended 1776).

1747

War of the Austrian Succession. Battle of Cape Finisterre (3 May):
  British fleet under Admiral Anson defeated French; Battle of
  Lauffeld (2 July): Austrians and British under the Duke of

Cumberland defeated by French under Marshal Saxe; Battle of Cape Finisterre (2 October): British fleet under Admiral Hawke defeated French.
Secession of the Society of Shakers from the Quakers.

1748

War of the Austrian Succession. Siege of French-held Pondicherry in India begun by British fleet and land forces (30 August); siege abandoned (October); Battle of Havana (12 October): indecisive naval battle between British and Spanish squadrons.
Henry Fielding appointed first British stipendiary magistrate.

1749

Carnatic War. Battle of Devicotta: capture of the fortress.
Halifax, Nova Scotia, founded: named in honour of George Montagu Dunk, 2nd Earl of Halifax.
Treaty of Aquisgran between Britain and Spain: commercial.
Publication of Henry Fielding's *Tom Jones*.
The Ohio Company, English colonizing organization, chartered.

1750

Bill for the Prohibition of Colonial Manufactures before Parliament.
Chiltern Hundreds first granted as grounds for resignation to MPs.
Publication of *Elegy* by Thomas Gray.
Beginning of manufacture of Bristol porcelain (ended 1880) and Derby porcelain.

c.1750

Invention of steel cast by the crucible process by Benjamin Huntsman.

1751

Carnatic War. Seizure (August) and defence of Arcot by Clive; Battle of Arnee: French force defeated by British and Maratha troops under Clive and treasure seized.
Manufacture of Doctor Wall (Worcester) porcelain began (ended 1783).

1752

Carnatic War. Battle of Chingleput: capture of French garrison by Clive.

Seven Years' War. Battle of Bahur (August): defeat of French and
   Indian troops in India by British and Muslim troops.
Britain adopted the Gregorian or New Style calendar (14 September),
   superseding the Julian or Old Style calendar, the eleven days being
   'lost', 3–11 September.
Last Stannary Parliament in Cornwall held at Truro.

1753

Carnatic War. Battle of Golden Rock (7 August): British defeated
   French; Battle of Sugar-Loaf Rock (20 September): successful
   British attack on French army besieging Trichinopoly; Battle of
   Seringham: British defeated French and Maratha forces.
British Museum founded (opened 16 January 1759).

1754

Newcastle ministry in Britain.
Carnatic War. Batte of Tondeman's Woods (14 February): supply
   convoy to Trichinopoly captured by Hyder Ali.
Prelude to Seven Years' War. Battle of Youghioghenny (27 May):
   American force under Washington attacked and defeated French.
Clandestine marriages abolished in England.
Foundation of the Royal Society of Arts.
Development of the theory of quantitive analysis by Joseph Black.
Modern form of the heliometer invented by John Dollond.
Foundation of the Royal and Ancient Golf Club of St Andrews.
Death of Henry Fielding (8 October).

1755

Convention of St Petersburg between Britain and Russia.
Prelude to Seven Years' War. Battle of Monongahela River (9 July):
   Braddock's force destroyed by French and Indians in America;
   Siege and capture of French fort at Beauséjour by British and
   Massachusetts volunteers (4–16 June); Battle of Lake George (8
   September): French attack defeated by New England militia.
Publication of *Dictionary of the English Language* by Dr Johnson.
Period of canal construction began (until 1827).

1756

Devonshire and Pitt (afterwards Earl of Chatham) formed a ministry
   (4 December).

Convention of Westminster between Britain and Prussia (16 January).

Britain declared war against France (15 May): Seven Years' War began (ended 1763). Calcutta besieged (16 June) by Surajah Dowlah and small British garrison seized (20 June); 146 survivors were detained in the 'Black Hole' (20-21 June): 23 survived; Minorca taken from the British by the French because of failure of British fleet under Byng; Siege and surrender of British at Oswego in North America to the French (11–14 August).

Publication of *A Philosophic Inquiry into the Origin of our Ideas of the Sublime and Beautiful* by Edmund Burke.

Construction of the Bridgewater Canal from Worsley to Manchester began (completed 1761).

Mortar developed by John Smeaton.

*c.*1756

Printing on porcelain developed in Liverpool and Worcester.

1757

Devonshire-Pitt cabinet fell (5 April). Ministry of Newcastle and Pitt (29 June). Coalition government.

First settlement of Tennessee, USA.

Seven Years' War. Clive captured Calcutta (2 January); Admiral Byng executed by firing squad at Portsmouth (14 March); Siege and capture of Chandernagore by Clive (14–24 March); Battle of Plassey between Lord Clive and Indian rebel forces (23 June): Clive 's victory over Surajah Dowlah; Battle of Hastenbeck (26 July): Hanoverians under Duke of Cumberland beaten by French; Siege and capture of British Fort William Henry (4–9 August): by French, Canadians and North American Indians; capitulation of British at Kloster Zeven (8 September).

1758

Seven Years' War. Battle of Ile d'Aix (4 March): French squadron defeated by British under Sir Edward Hawke; French expedition to North America delayed; Battle of Fort St David (29 April): naval battle in India between French and British fleets; outcome indecisive; Second Battle of Fort St David in India (14 May): successful siege of British fortress by French forces; British captured Louisburg (8 June) with troops and fleet; Battle of Ticonderoga (8 July): British attack on French under Montcalm failed; Battle of

Carrical (2 August): engagement of British and French fleets off the coast of India; outcome indecisive; Battle of Fort Frontenac (27 August): British gained control of Lake Ontario from French; Battle of Grant's Hill (14 September): British forces defeated by French; Battle of Rajahmundry (9 December): British defeated French; Battle of Madras (16 December): Madras regained from the French; Clive became Governor of Bengal.

Appearance of Halley's Comet (named after Edmund Halley).

1759

Seven Years' War. Siege and capture of the French at Masulipatam north of Madras by the British (March); Siege of Quebec by British under General Wolfe began (27 June); Siege and capture of French fort at Niagara by British (24 July); Battle of Montmorenci in North America (31 July): British attack on French position defeated; Battle of Minden (1 August): French defeated; Battle of Trincomalee (10 August): inconclusive naval engagement between British and French fleets off India; Battle of Quebec (Battle of the Heights of Abraham) (13 September): Britain defeated French; Wolfe and Montcalm both killed; Quebec surrendered (17 September); Battle of Quiberon Bay (20 November): British fleet under Hawke annihilated French fleet.

Anglo-Dutch Conflict in India. Battle of Hooghly (24 November): Dutch ships and troops defeated by British in India.

Kew Gardens, London, established by Princess Augusta, Dowager Princess of Wales.

Opening of the British Museum to the public (15 January).

Completion of the third Eddystone Lighthouse (designed by John Smeaton).

Invention of a ribbing machine for the manufacture of stockings by Jedediah Strutt.

Death of the composer Handel (14 April).

1760

Death of George II (25 October): his grandson became king of Britain as George III.

Seven Years' War. Battle of Wandiwash (22 January): British under Sir Eyre Coote defeated French in India; Siege of Pondicherry began; Battle of Ste Foy (27 April): British defeated by French;

Battle of Quebec: French laid siege to Quebec; siege abandoned after arrival of British squadron that cut the French lines of supply (16 May); Capitulation of Montreal: Britain master of Canada; Battle of Warburg (31 July): French defeated by British and Prussians.

First British school for the deaf and dumb set up in Edinburgh by Thomas Braidwood.

Laurence, Earl Ferrers executed by hanging (5 May): last nobleman to be executed in Britain; first use of hangman's drop.

1761

Marriage of George III and Princess Charlotte Sophia of Mecklenburg-Strelitz.

Fall of Pitt. Bute became prime minister.

Seven Years' War. Pondicherry surrendered to British (15 January).

Opening of the Bridgewater Canal (17 July).

1762

Birth of a son (later Prince Regent and George IV) to George III (12 August).

Britain declared war against Spain (4 January).

Seven Years' War. Siege and capture of Havana by British (5 June); Manila, Martinique, etc, also captured by Britain. Battle of Wilhelmsthal: British and Hanoverian victory over France. Battle of Lutternberg: British and Hanoverians defeated the French.

First demonstration of the compressibility of water by John Canton.

Cigars introduced into Britain from Cuba.

*c.*1762

Cheques issued by English banker Lawrence Childe.

1763

Bute resigned office in Britain: Grenville ministry formed (7 April).

Beginning of Pontiac's Rebellion (ended 1764) led by Pontiac, American Indian chief.

Conquest of Bengal. Battle of Morshedabad (24 July): British defeated the deposed Nawab of Bengal and occupied the city; British captured Bengali fort at Oondwa Nullah (September).

Whiteboy outbreaks in Ireland.

Seven Years' War ended by Peace of Hubertusburg between Prussia,

Austria and Saxony (15 February), and Treaty of Paris between France, Spain and Britain (10 February): Britain gained Canada, Nova Scotia, Cape Breton, St Vincent, Dominica, Tobago, Grenada, etc, regained Minorca; Pondicherry restored to French; Illinois ceded by France to Britain; Ontario, Canada, became British territory.

Almack's club (established as Brooks's 1778) founded by William Almack (d.1781).

1764

John Wilkes expelled from House of Commons (19 January)..
Battle of Buxar: Britain gained Oude, etc.
Latent existence of heat established by Joseph Black.
Lloyd's Register of shipping first prepared.

c.1764

Invention of the spinning jenny by James Hargreaves.

1765

Birth of a third son (later William IV) to George III and Queen Charlotte (21 August).
Stamp Act passed by British Parliament (23 March, repealed 1766).
Rockingham Ministry formed (16 July, until 1766).
First volume published of *Blackstone's Commentaries,* legal guide by Sir William Blackstone (completed 1769).
Opening of Sadler's Wells Theatre, London (reconstruction 1879; closure 1916; reopening 1931).

1766

Repeal of Stamp Act (11 March), but Declaratory Act passed declaring Britain's right to tax the colonies.
Chatham and Grafton formed Ministry, Chatham prime minister (12 July, until 1767).
Isle of Man became a Crown Colony.
North Dakota first settled.
Falkland Islands occupied by British.
Christie's auctioneers founded and had first sale (5 December).
Publication of Oliver Goldsmith's *Vicar of Wakefield.*
Construction of the Grand Trunk Canal began by James Brindley.
Death in Rome of the 'Old Pretender', James Stewart (1 January).

1767

Tea and other duties imposed by British Parliament on America (May).

First Mysore War. Battle of Trincomalee (3 September): British withstood attack by Hyder Ali; Battle of Trincomalee (26 September); British defeated Hyder Ali; Siege of Ambur by Hyder Ali began (10 November); relieved (6 December).

British Nautical Almanac first published.

Newcomen's steam pumping engine perfected by James Watt.

Discovery of Pitcairn Island in the Pacific Ocean by Philip Carteret.

Discovery of Tahiti by Captain Wallis.

1768

Chatham retired: Grafton head of ministry.

First Mysore War. Attack at Ooscata by Hyder Ali repulsed (23 August).

Establishment of the Royal Academy (10 December): its first president was Joshua Reynolds.

The water spinning frame invented by English inventor Arkwright.

Beginning of Captain Cook's first voyage (ended 1771).

Death of the novelist Laurence Sterne (18 March).

1769

First of *Letters of Junius* published.

First practical boring machine invented by John Smeaton.

Cook's expedition reached New Zealand (7 October).

1770

Lord North became prime minister (until 1782) after resignation of Grafton (28 January).

Spaniards attacked British in Falkland Islands. Falkland Islands ceded to Britain by Spain (January).

The 'Boston Massacre' (5 March): five rioters killed in Boston, Massachusetts by British troops.

Foundation of the Radcliffe Observatory, Oxford University, by the executors of John Radcliffe.

Astley's Circus founded by Philip Astley.

Burke published *Thoughts on the Present Discontents*.

Portland Vase, Roman funerary urn (now in the British Museum), bought by Sir William Hamilton.

Manufacture of Chelsea-Derby porcelain began (ended 1784).
Botany Bay, New South Wales, discovered (28 April) by Captain Cook.
  Captain Cook declared New South Wales as British (23 August).
Cook Strait, New Zealand, discovered by Captain Cook.
First crossing of Barren Grounds, Canada, begun by Samuel Hearne
  (completed 1772).
Discovery of Lake Tana in Ethiopia as the source of the Blue Nile by
  James Bruce (14 November).
The poet Thomas Chatterton committed suicide.

1772

Royal Marriage Act.
Slavery declaed illegal in Britain.
Discovery of nitrogen by Daniel Rutherford.
Laughing gas (nitrous oxide) discovered by Joseph Priestley (first
  used as an anaesthetic 1844).
Manufacture of Caughley porcelain began (ended 1799).
Beginning of Captain Cook's second voyage (ended 1775).

1773

Indian Regulating Act passed concerning East India Company.
Warren Hastings became first governor-general of Bengal.
First Mysore War. Siege and capture of fortress of Tanjore by British
  troops (20 August–16 September).
Boston Tea Party, American revolutionary protest against unfair
  British taxation (16 December).

1774

Hansard record of parliamentary debates begun by Luke Hansard.
Retaliatory legislation to Boston Tea Party by British Parliament (28
  March). The first Continental Congress met in Philadelphia to
  protest at the repressive British legislation.
Quebec Act passed concerning the territory and government of the
  Province of Quebec.
Battle of Point Pleasant between American Indians and the Virginia
  militia (10 October).
Warren Hastings became first governor-general of India (until 1785).
Oxygen and ammonia gas discovered by Joseph Priestley.
Discovery of New Caledonia in the South Pacific by Captain Cook
  (annexed by France 1853).

Discovery of Norfolk Island in the South Pacific by Captain Cook.
Lord Clive committed suicide (22 November).

1775

First Maratha War. Battle of Aras (18 May): British defeated the
  Marathas.
War of American Independence began (ended 1783). Battle of
  Lexington (19 April): American victory; Washington became
  commander-in-chief of American troops (15 June); Battle of Bunker
  Hill (17 June): Americans defeated.
Commercial steam engines produced by Watt and Boulton.

1776

Parliament passed a Prohibitory Act against American commerce.
War of American Independence. Americans forced out of Canada
  (March); Declaration of Independence by American colonies (4
  July).
Edward Gibbon began publication of his *Decline and Fall of the
  Roman Empire.*
Publication of Adam Smith's *Wealth of Nations.*
The properties of hydrogen discovered by Henry Cavendish.
Beginning of Captain Cook's third voyage (11 July, ended 1779).
Foundation of Tattersall's horse auction and sporting centre by
  Richard Tattersall.
St Leger horse race first run at Doncaster.
Death of David Hume.

1777

War of American Independence. Battle of Princeton (3 January):
  British under Cornwallis defeated by Americans under Washington;
  British siege and capture of fortress of Ticonderoga (22 June–5
  July); Battle of Brandywine (11 September); British defeated
  Americans and seized Wilmington; Battle of Germantown (3
  October): British defeated Americans; Battle of Stillwater or Battle
  of Saratoga (7–17 October): British under General Burgoyne
  defeated by Americans; Burgoyne surrendered.
Suspension of the Habeas Corpus Act (February).
First performance of *School for Scandal* by Richard Sheridan (8
  May).
Christmas Island discovered by Captain Cook.

1778

Roman Catholic Relief Act passed.

Treaty of Paris between France and America (6 February). Treaty between Holland and America.

War of American Independence. Battle of Carenage Bay: French fleet defeated by the British; the British seized St Lucia; Battle of Monmouth in New Jersey (28 June): British defeated by Washington; Battle of Onessant (27 July): inconclusive naval battle between British and French squadrons; Battle of Pondicherry (10 August) British naval defeat of French; Pondicherry captured by the British (September).

Discovery of the Sandwich Islands (later Hawaii) by Captain Cook (18 January).

Deaths: the composer Thomas Arne (5 March); William Pitt the Elder, Earl of Chatham (11 May).

1779

First Maratha War. Battle of Wargaom (12 January): British withstood Maratha attack.

Irish Volunteers first formed.

War of American Independence. Spain declared war against Britain 16 June); Siege of Gibraltar began (relieved 1783); Battle of Grenada (6 July): unsuccessful British naval attempt to regain Grenada from French; Battle of Penobscot Bay (14 July): British squadron defeated American squadron.

Construction completed (began 1773) of the first iron bridge at Coalbrookdale, Ironbridge, Shropshire.

Spinning mule (Crompton's mule) invented by Samuel Crompton.

Murder of Captain Cook in the Sandwich Islands (14 February).

The Oaks horse race first run at Epsom.

Deaths: the actor David Garrick (20 January); the cabinet-maker Thomas Chippendale.

1780

First Maratha War. British took fortresses at Ahmadabad (15 February) and Gwalior (3 August); British massacred by Tippu Sahib at Perembacum (10 September); British besieged and captured Bassein (13–14 November); British defeated Marathas at Deeg.

Armed Neutrality formed against Britain by Russia and Prussia (10 March).

War of American Independence: Charleston taken by British (May); Battle of Camden (16 August): the British under General Cornwallis defeated the Americans.

First Mysore War. Siege of British at Tellicherry began (June); attack by Tippu Sahib defeated by British at Ponani (19 November); Siege of British fort at Wandiwash began (December).

Gordon Riots occurred (2-9 June), instigated by a petition against the Roman Catholic Relief Act led by Lord George Gordon.

Britain declared war against Holland (20 November).

Foundation of Bampton Lectures at Oxford University, by John Bampton: annual series.

Rebuilt Fleet Prison destroyed.

Foundation of Sunday schools by Robert Raikes.

Foundation of the Society of Antiquaries of Scotland.

Hectograph duplicating process invented by James Watt.

Introduction of the willow pattern on pottery by Thomas Turner.

The Derby horse race first run at Epsom (4 May).

1781

First Mysore War. Siege of Wandiwash lifted by Hyder Ali after arrival of British reinforcements (22 January); Battle of Porto Novo (1 July): British under Sir Eyre Coote advancing on Cuddalore defeated Hyder Ali; Battle of Pollicore (27 August): British defeated Mysore troops under Hyder Ali; Battle of Sholingur (27 September): British defeated Hyder Ali; Siege and capture of Mysore garrison (21 October–3 November).

War of American Independence. Battle of Guildford Courthouse (15 March): British victory over Americans; Battle of Cape Henry (16 March): French fleet defeated by British fleet; Battle of Porto Praia Bay, Cape Verde (16 April): French attack on British squadron defeated; Battle of Dogger Bank (15 August): British fleet defeated by Dutch; Battle of Chesapeake Bay (5 September): British defeated by French; Battle of Lynn Haven Bay (5 September): failure of British naval attack on French fleet; Battle of Eutaw Springs (8 September): futile victory of British over Americans; Siege of Yorktown (September): Cornwallis surrendered to Washington (19 October).

Discovery of the planet Uranus by William Herschel (13 March).
Manufacture of Worcester porcelain began.

1782

Resignation of Lord North (19 March); second Rockingham ministry
  formed. Death of Rockingham (1 July); succeeded by Shelburne.
  Coalition government.
First Maratha War ended by Treaty of Salbai (17 May).
First Mysore War. British reinforcements relieved Tellicherry (18
  January); Battle of Arnee (7 June) between British under Sir Eyre
  Coote and Mysore troops under Hyder Ali: outcome indecisive;
  death of Hyder Ali (7 December); succeeded by Tippu Sahib.
Ireland. Declaration of Rights by Grattan: Irish legislative independ-
  ence; Repeal of Poynings' Law.
War of American Independence. Minorca taken from British by Spain
  (5 February); Battle of Dominica (12 April): British fleet defeated
  French, Rodney's victory saving Jamaica; Battle of Trincomalee (12
  April): inconclusive naval battle between British and French fleets
  off India; Battle of Pondicherry (20 June): inconclusive naval battle
  between French and British; Battle of Trincomalee (3 September):
  second inconclusive battle between British and French fleets.
Sinking of *The Royal George* at Portsmouth.
Fleet Prison rebuilt.
James Watt patented his steam engine.

1783

Resignation of Shelburne (24 April); coalition ministry of Portland,
  Fox and North; Fox's India Bill rejected by the House of Lords;
  William Pitt in power (19 December, until 1801): at twenty-four
  Britain's youngest prime minister.
First Mysore War. Siege of British garrison at Mangalore begun by
  Tippu Sahib.
War of American Independence. Battles of Cuddalore in India: First
  (13 June) British defeated French and took Cuddalore; Second (20
  June): British fleet unable to secure sea access to Cuddalore; Treaty
  of Versailles between Britain, France, Spain and America, ending
  the War of American Independence (3 September): Britain recog-
  nized independence of American colonies; St Vincent and other
  West Indian possessions ceded to Britain by France, who recovered

possession in the east. Spain kept Minorca; Bahamas became
  British colony (until 1964).
First Chamber of Commerce in Britain founded in Glasgow.
Foundation of the Order of St Patrick by George III.
Completion of the rebuilding of Newgate Prison in London (begun
  1770).
Death of Capability Brown, landscape gardener (6 February).

1784

Dissolution of parliament (4 March); after elections Pitt in power
  with large majority.
  India Act of William Pitt established control of the East India
  Company by the government (August).
First Mysore War. British garrison at Mangalore surrendered to Tippu
  Sahib.
Peace of Versailles between England and Holland (20 May).
First balloon ascent in Britain.
Invention of the puddling furnace by Henry Cort.
Invention of the threshing machine by Andrew Meikle.
Mail coaches first ran, between London and Bristol (2 August).
Imposition of a tax on bricks (lifted 1850).
The Honourable Company of Edinburgh Golfers, the first golf club,
  founded.
Death of the writer and lexicographer Dr Samuel Johnson (13
  December).

1785

Resignation of Warren Hastings and return to England (June).
Home Office founded by now.
Marriage of the Prince of Wales (later George IV) and Mrs Maria
  Fitzherbert (15 December); marriage invalid but they remained
  together until 1811.
Penang, peninsular Malaysia, ceded to the East India Company by the
  Sultan of Kedah.
Foundation of *The Times* by John Walter (adopted present name
  1788).
First balloon crossing of the English Channel by Blanchard and
  Jeffries (7 January).

First lifeboat designed by Lionel Lukin, English coach-builder.
The power loom invented by Edmund Cartwright.

1786

Commercial Treaty between Britain and France (26 September).
Botany Bay became British penal settlement for transportation.
Robert Burns published first volume of poems (9 December).
The existence of the Indo-European language postulated by Sir
  William Jones.
Manufacture of Chamberlain porcelain (ended 1840).
Death of George Hepplewhite, English cabinetmaker.

1787

Impeachment of Warren Hastings by Edmund Burke.
First English settlement in Sierra Leone.
MCC (Marylebone Cricket Club) founded (first match held 1788).

1788

First motion in House of Commons for abolition of slave trade.
King George III suffered a serious bout of insanity (probably caused
  by the disease porphyria).
Trial for impeachment of Warren Hastings for corruption (February).
Triple Alliance between Britain, Holland and Prussia.
First transported convicts to Australia arrived at Sydney (26 January).
Publication of *The Times* began (1 January), replacing *The Daily
  Universal Register*.
Publication completed of *The Decline and Fall of the Roman Empire*
  (begun 1766) by Edward Gibbon.
Completion of first steam flour meal, at Blackfriars, London, by John
  Rennie (burned down 1791).
Linnean Society, London, founded by James Smith.
Deaths: Bonnie Prince Charlie in Rome (31 January); the painter
  Thomas Gainsborough (2 August).

1789

Second Mysore War. Battle of Travancore (28 December): British
  troops withstood attack by Tippu Sahib.
Mutiny of the crew of the *Bounty* led by Fletcher Christian against
  Captain Bligh (28 April).
British attacked by Spaniards at Nootka Sound, British Columbia (June).

Publication of *The Natural History and Antiquities of Selbourne* by
Gilbert White.

Publication of William Blake's *Songs of Innocence*.

1790

Second Mysore War. Battle of Calicut (10 December): British victory
over Mysore troops led by Hussein Ali.

Berlin Convention of England, Holland and Prussia regarding
Belgium (9 January).

Nootka Sound Convention between Britain and Spain (28 October).

Mutineers from the *Bounty* settled on Pitcairn Island.

Publication of *Reflections on the Revolution in France* by Burke.

Forth and Clyde Canal completed (begun 1768) by John Smeaton.

Manufacture of Coalport porcelain began.

Deaths: John Howard from jail fever in Russia; the economist Adam
Smith (17 July).

1791

Split in the Whigs.

Constitutional Act for Canada (6 May); Ontario organized as Upper
Canada.

Ireland. Wolfe Tone founded the Society of United Irishmen.

Second Mysore War. Battle of Arikera or Carigat (13 May): Tippu
Sahib defeated by British troops under General Lord Cornwallis.

Establishment of the Ordnance Survey of Great Britain.

Joseph Priestley's house in Birmingham burned down by mob.

First publication of *The Observer* newspaper, the oldest Sunday
newspaper (4 December).

Thomas Paine's *Rights of Man* and Sir James Mackintosh's *Vindiciae
Gallicae*: replies to Burke's *Reflections*.

Discovery of titanium (under the name menachinite) by Rev. William
Gregor: named titanium 1795.

Deaths: Selina Hastings, Countess of Huntingdon, founder of the
'Countess of Huntingdon's Connexion', a Calvinist-Methodist sect
(now part of the United Reformed Church); John Wesley (2 March).

1792

Second Mysore War. Siege of Seringapatam begun (5 February) by
British and Indian troops led by Lord Cornwallis; Tippu Sahib
surrendered (16 February); end of war (March).

Introduction of money orders in Britain (1 October).

Completion of publication (began 1791) of *The Rights of Man* by
    Thomas Paine.

Publication of Mary Wollstonecraft's *Rights of Women*.

Coal-gas lighting invented by William Murdock.

Deaths: Sir Joshua Reynolds (23 February); the architect Robert
    Adam (3 March); Lord North (5 August).

1793

First Coalition of Allies against France. France declared war against
    Britain and Holland (1 February).

French Revolutionary Wars. Toulon surrendered to Admiral Hood (28
    August). French besieged and recovered Toulon (18 December):
    Napoleon Bonaparte distinguished himself; British took Tobago
    from the French.

£5 notes first issued by the Bank of England (15 April).

First free settlers arrived in New South Wales.

William Godwin's *Political Justice*.

Manufacture of Davenant porcelain began (ended 1882).

Death of Lord George Gordon in prison (1 November).

1794

Suspension of Habeas Corpus Act for eight years.

William Pitt's coalition with the Portland Whigs.

French Revolutionary Wars. Treaty of the Hague between Britain,
    Holland and Prussia (19 April); Battle of the Glorious First of June
    or Battle of Ushant (1 June): British fleet under Howe defeated the
    French fleet; island of St Lucia taken from French by British fleet (4
    April); Battle of Tourcoing (17 May): British under Duke of York
    defeated by the French; Battle of Guadeloupe (3 July): island of
    Guadeloupe gained from the French by a British force; recaptured
    by French (10 December); Prussia withdrew from Treaty of the Hague.

The Gordon Highlanders raised.

Publication of *The Mysteries of Udolpho* by Mrs Radcliffe.

Third Drury Lane Theatre in London opened.

Death of Edward Gibbon (16 January).

1795

Marriage of the Prince of Wales (later George IV) and Princess
    Caroline of Brunswick.

Warren Hastings acquitted (23 April).

Ireland. Orange Society (Orangemen), Irish Protestant association, founded in Ireland.

French Revolutionary Wars. Triple Alliance of Britain, Austria and Russia; French troops conquered Holland and established the Batavian Republic; British took Ceylon and Malacca from Dutch (February); French recaptured St Lucia (June); Cape Town taken by British from Dutch (September).

The consumption of lime juice made compulsory in the Royal Navy as a preventative of scurvy.

Navigation of the River Niger by Mungo Park.

Death of James Boswell (19 May).

1796

Birth of a daughter, Princess Charlotte, to the Prince of Wales and Princess Caroline. The Prince of Wales deserted Caroline, and she went to live abroad.

French Revolutionary Wars. Saldanha Bay taken from the Dutch by the British (17 August); British evacuated Corsica; British reconquered St Lucia from French and took Demerara from the Dutch; Spain declared war on Britain (5 October); French under Hoche attempted the invasion of Ireland at Bantry Bay but failed (December).

Revival of vaccination against smallpox by Edward Jenner (14 May).

Semaphore signalling developed by Lord George Murray.

The carbon composition of diamonds demonstrated by Smithson Tennant.

The hydraulic press invented by Joseph Bramah.

Death of Robert Burns (21 July).

1797

Cash payments suspended in Britain.

French Revolutionary Wars. Battle of Cape St Vincent (14 February): Spanish fleet defeated by Jervis; Britain took Trinidad from France (17 February); Battle of Camperdown (11 October): Dutch fleet on its way to link up with the French to land in Ireland defeated by British fleet under Admiral Duncan.

Mutiny in British fleet at Spithead (16 April): demands granted.

Mutiny in British fleet at the Nore against poor pay and conditions, led by Richard Parker (23 May–30 June): special legislation against it. Parker hanged.

£1 banknotes issued for the first time by the Bank of England (26 February).

The mass of the Earth first calculated by Henry Cavendish.

Deaths: Edmund Burke (9 July); John Wilkes (26 December).

1798

Irish Rebellion. Battle of Ballymore (3 June): Irish rebels attacked and defeated English force; Battle of New Ross (5 June): rebel attack defeated; Battle of Arklow (9 June): rebel attack repulsed; Battle of Vinegar Hill (21 June): British under General Lake attacked Irish rebels and defeated them; death by suicide of Wolfe Tone.

French Revolutionary Wars. Bonaparte's Egyptian expedition set sail; Malta taken by French (12 June); Battle of the Pyramids (21 July): French victory in Egypt; Bonaparte entered Cairo; Battle of the Nile or Battle of Aboukir Bay (1 August): British under Nelson destroyed French fleet under Brueys; Siege of Valletta in Malta by British and Maltese began (September); French invasion of Ireland failed (27 October); Minorca captured by British (November); Alliance between Russia and Britain (24 December).

Publication of Malthus's *Essay on the Principle of Population*.

Lyrical Ballads of Wordsworth and Coleridge.

Bass Strait between Australia and Tasmania discovered by George Bass.

Bleaching powder discovered by Smithson Tennant.

First planned human experiment to test an hypothesis based on observation undertaken by Edward Jenner.

Death of the explorer George Vancouver (10 May).

1799

Income tax introduced in Britain by Pitt (9 January).

Repressive legislation in Britain against political associations and combinations (12 July).

Third Mysore War. Attacks by Tippu Sahib on British forces at Sidassir (6 March) and Malavilly (20 March) repulsed; British stormed Seringapatam (3 May): Tippu Sahib, sultan of Mysore, killed.

French Revolutionary Wars/Napoleonic Wars. Battle of Bergen:
  British and Russians defeated in Holland; Battle of Novi between
  the Allies and the French (15 August); Battle of Alkmaar (2
  October): British and Russian troops under the Duke of York
  defeated the French; Convention of Alkmaar: Britain to evacuate
  Holland; British took Surinam from Dutch.
Foundation of Sandhurst Royal Military College by the Duke of York.
Foundation of the Royal Institution of Great Britain.

1800

Union of Britain and Ireland under the Act of Union as the United
  Kingdom (Great Britain) (2 July): abolition of Irish Parliament.
The province of Wellesley, peninsular Malaysia, added to Penang.
French Revolutionary Wars/Napoleonic Wars. British captured Malta
  from the French (12 June); Siege of Valletta ended (5 September).
Russia, Prussia, Denmark and Sweden form Northern Confederacy
  against Britain (16 December).
Mutiny of the *Danae*.
Foundation of the Royal College of Surgeons.
Beginning of Robert Owen's social reforms at New Lanark.
First shipment of the Elgin Marbles brought from the Parthenon in
  Athens to London by Lord Elgin (completed 1803).
Electric light first produced by Sir Humphry Davy.
Use of high-pressure steam pioneered by Richard Trevithick.

1801

The Act of Union became effective (1 January).
Pitt resigned: Addington became prime minister.
Madras state in India brought under British rule by now.
Napoleonic Wars. Battle of Aboukir (8 March): British troops under
  Abercromby landed at Aboukir in Egypt and defeated French
  troops; Battle of Alexandria (21 March): Abercromby defeated
  French, but killed: Cairo surrendered to British: French evacuated
  Egypt. Battle of Copenhagen between the British and Danish fleets
  (2 April): Nelson destroyed Danish fleet, using his blind eye not to
  see the signal to break of the fight; Battle of Algeçiras Bay (8 July):
  naval battle between the French and British.
Dissolution of the Northern Confederacy. Treaty of St Petersburg

between Russia and Britain.

Publication of the first census made in Britain (29 June).

The element columbium (niobium) isolated by Charles Hatchett.

1802

Ceylon became a British colony.

Treaty of Bassein between Britain and the Peshwa: led to Second
  Maratha War.

Treaty of Amiens between Great Britain, France, Spain and the
  Netherlands (25 March): an unstable settlement; Minorca returned
  to Spain.

First British Factory Act.

Edinburgh Review founded (October): organ of Whigs.

Charlotte Dundas, the first practicable steamboat, built by William
  Symington.

1803

Cobbett began unofficial publication of Parliamentary reports
  (publication taken over by Hansard report 1811).

Second Maratha War. Battle of Aligarh (29 August): capture of the
  fortress and arsenal by British troops; Battle of Delhi (11 September): British victory; Battle of Assaye (23 September): British and
  Indian troops won a bloody victory; Siege of Agra began (4
  October): British troops besieged the fortress; the garrison surrendered (18 October); Battle of Laswari (1 November): Sind's army
  defeated by British under General Lake; Battle of Argaon (28
  November): Wellesley (later Duke of Wellington) defeated the
  Marathas.

Orissa, India, conquered by the British.

Balearic Islands ceded to Spain by the British.

Britain declared war against France.

First publication of *Debrett's Peerage* by John Debrett.

Dalton's Law of partial pressures defined by John Dalton.

Discovery of the metallic element osmium by Smithson Tennant and
  of the metallic elements palladium and rhodium by William
  Wollaston.

Early locomotive constructed by Richard Trevithick. Opening of the
  first public railway (Wandsworth to Croydon).

Semaphore signalling perfected by Admiral Popham.

Execution of Edward Despard for Despard's Plot against the British government.

Robert Emmet, Irish rebel, hanged (20 September).

1804

Pitt again prime minister (until 1805).

Second Maratha War. Battle of Delhi (7–16 October): Maratha siege of British garrison was unsuccessful; Battle of Farrukhabad (14 November): defeat of Marathas; Battle of Deeg (11–23 December): British siege successful.

Napoleonic Wars. Battle of Surinam (5 May): British captured Dutch garrison. Napoleon made Spain declare war against Britain (12 December).

Foundation of the Royal Society of Painters in Watercolours.

Construction of the Caledonian Canal across Scotland by Thomas Telford began (completed 1822).

Discovery of iridium by Smithson Tennant.

Opening of the Rochdale canal, constructed by John Rennie.

Establishment of the first savings bank at Rotherham.

Death of the scientist Joseph Priestley (6 February).

1805

Napoleonic Wars. Battle of Cape Finisterre (22 July): Franco-Spanish fleet under Villeneuve defeated by British fleet under Admiral Sir Robert Calder; Battle of Trafalgar between the British and the Franco-Spanish fleet (21 October): Nelson destroyed Franco-Spanish fleet but killed in the action.

Armour plate first proposed for ships of war by Sir William Congreve.

Trooping of the Colour first held in London (4 June).

Endowment to Oxford University of the Newdigate Prize for English verse by Sir Roger Newdigate.

Sir Walter Scott's Lay *of the Last Minstrel.*

Completion of the Grand Junction Canal (begun 1793).

The percussion detonator for firearms invented by the Scottish minister Alexander Forsyth.

1806

Death of William Pitt the Younger (23 January): Ministry of 'All the Talent' formed (resigned 1807) under Grenville and including Fox.

Napoleonic Wars. New Treaty between France and Prussia. Prussia

compelled to exclude British ships from Prussian ports: Britain
declared war against Prussia; British occupied Buenos Aires, but
forced by townspeople to surrender; Battle of Maida (6 July):
British defeated French in southern Italy. Berlin Decrees (21
November): beginning of the imposition of the Continental System
closing continental ports against British imports.
Carbon paper patented by Ralph Wedgwood (7 October).
Death of Charles James Fox (13 September).

1807
Tory ministry of Portland and Perceval.
Bill passed by British Parliament abolishing the slave trade.
Napoleonic Wars. British Order in Council in reply to Berlin Decrees.
  British captured Montevideo (3 February) and then retroceded it;
  Russia and Prussia joined the Continental System (July); British
  captured island of Heligoland from Denmark (31 August); British
  bombardment and capture of Copenhagen (5 September): Danish
  fleet surrendered; Milan Decree issued by Napoleon extending ban
  on British goods (7 December); the Caribbean islands of St Thomas
  and Ste Croix taken from the Danish by a British military and naval
  force (21 and 25 December).
Downing College, Cambridge, built.
Discovery of potassium and sodium by Humphry Davy.
Distinction between sensory and motor nerves made by Charles Bell.
First recorded journey of the Mumbles Railway, Swansea, the oldest
  British passenger railway (closed 1 January 1960).
Shore-to-ship lifeline, fired by mortar, invented by George Manby.
Ascot Gold Cup horse race initiated.

1808
Sierra Leone became a British colony (until 1960).
Peninsular War between the Allies and Napoleon (ended 1814);
  British force landed in Portugal under Wellington; Battle of Rolica
  (17 August): British and Portuguese under Wellington defeated
  French; Battle of Vimiero (21 August): Wellington defeated Junot;
  Battle of Espinosa (10 November): French victory over Spanish
  troops under General Blake.
Discovery of the elements barium, boron, calcium, magnesium and
  strontium by Sir Humphry Davy.

1809

Perceval became prime minister (until 1812).

Signature of friendship treaty between British and Sikhs (25 April).

Napoleonic Wars. USA brought in legislation against trade with Britain (January); Martinique taken from the French by the British (24 February); Walcheren Expedition (28 July–23 December): British besieged Flushing, which surrendered (16 August), but expedition to take Antwerp failed; Austria joined Continental System (14 October).

Peninsular War. Battle of Corunna (16 January): French attack to prevent embarkation of British army defeated by General Moore; Moore was killed; French under Marshal Soult took Oporto (28 March); Battle of Douro (12 May): Wellington drove Soult out of Oporto; Battle of Talavera between the French and the English (27-28 July): French under Victor defeated by Wellington.

Opening of Dartmoor Prison (24 May), originally for French prisoners of war.

Christian Tract Society founded by Robert Aspland.

The *Quarterly Review* founded by John Murray: organ of the Tories.

Study of aerodynamics founded by Sir George Cayley.

The Two Thousand Guineas horse race first run at Newmarket.

Death of Thomas Paine in New York (8 June).

1810

Napoleonic Wars. Sweden joined Continental System (January); Battle of Ile de France (3 December): Mauritius taken from the French by the British.

Peninsular War. Battle of Busaco (27 September): Wellington defeated Massena; Coimbra with its garrison taken by British; Wellington retired behind the lines of Torres Vedras; Fontainebleau Decrees by Napoleon against British goods (October).

Foundation of the Independent Order of Oddfellows temperance society in Manchester.

The Luddites, machine wreckers, active (until 1818).

Chiswick Press founded in London by Charles Whittingham.

First British landing on Rockall Island, off the Outer Hebrides.

c.1810

Orange Free State, South Africa, first settled.

1811

George III incapacited by insanity: the Prince of Wales, later George IV, became Prince Regent.

Sir George Prevost became governor-general of Canada (until 1816).

Peninsular War. Battle of Sabugal (3 April): British under Wellington defeated French; Battle of Fuentes D'Oñoro (8 May): Massena failed against Wellington; Wellington took Almeida; Battle of Albuera (16 May): Allied armies under Sir William Beresford defeated French under Marshal Soult; Siege of Tarragona completed by the French (28 June); attacks by French on British-held fortress of Sagunto failed (23 September, 18 October); besieged by French and surrendered (26 October); Russia and Britain agreed secretly to break the Continental System (December).

Appearance of the Primitive Methodist sect.

Bell Rock Lighthouse completed (begun 1807).

First ichthyosaurus to be brought to scientific notice by Mary Anning.

First county cricket match played by women (3 October).

1812

Assassination of Spencer Perceval by Francis Bellingham in the House of Commons (11 May): Liverpool became prime minister (until 1827).

Manitoba organized as the Red River Settlement.

War of 1812 between Britain and the United States. USA declared war on Britain (18 June); Battle of Queenston Heights (13 October): severe defeat of the Americans.

Peninsular War. Wellington besieged and captured Ciudad Rodrigo (8–15 March); Battle of Badajoz: attack began (17 March 1812) on fortress by Wellington's army and Portuguese troops; fortress and town captured (7 April), enabling Wellington's advance into Spain; Battle of Salamanca (22 July): British under Wellington defeated French under Marmont; Wellington entered Madrid (12 August).

Fourth Drury Lane Theatre in London opened.

Publication of *Childe Harold's Pilgrimage* by Lord Byron.

First gas company, the Gas Light and Coke Company, granted charter.

Goodwood Cup first run.

*c.*1812

Gas lighting first used as street lighting.

1813

Formation of the Quadruple Alliance of the Allies (Austria, Britain, Prussia and Russia) against Napoleon.

Peninsular War. Battle of Castella (13 April): Allied troops under Sir John Murray defeated French under Marshal Suchet; Battle of Vittoria (21 June): Allied troops under Wellington defeated French under Marshal Jourdan and King Joseph Bonaparte; Siege and capture of San Sebstian by the British (10–31 July); French-held citadel surrendered (9 September); Battle of Colde Maya (25 July): French defeat of British; Battles of the Pyrenees: (25 July–2 August): Wellington defeated Soult; Battle of Dennewitz (6 September): French defeated; Battle of Nivelle (10 November): Wellington defeated French; Battle of the Nive (13 December): British and Portuguese under Wellington defeated French under Marshal Soult; Wellington invaded France (22 December).

War of 1812. Battle between the British frigate *Shannon* and the American *Chesapeake* (29 May); Battle of Lake Erie (10 September): American fleet defeated a British fleet; Battle of Chrysler's Farm (11 November): British defeat of American force; British forced out of Detroit.

Napoleonic Wars. Battle of Leipzig (Battle of the Nations) (16-19 October): Napoleon defeated by the Allies; Leipzig taken.

Publication of *Pride and Prejudice* by Jane Austen.

Invention of 'Puffing Billy', pioneer locomotive by William Hedley.

1814

Peninsular War. Battle of Orthez (27 February): British under Wellington defeated French under Soult.

Napoleonic Wars. Battle of Craonne (7 March): French defeat of Allied armies; Treaty of Chaumont between Russia, Austria, Prussia, and Britain (9 March); Battle of Laon (10 March): Allies defeated Napoleon; Battle of Arcis-sur-Aube (20 March): French defeated by Allied armies; Allies occupied Paris (March 31); Battle of Toulouse (10 April): Wellington defeated Soult; abdication of Napoleon (11 April); Treaty of Paris (Treaty of Fontainebleau), ending the Napoleonic Wars, accepted by Napoleon: banished to Elba (April 13); renewal of the Quadruple Alliance of the Allies (Austria, Britain, Prussia and Russia) against Napoleon (20 November).

War of 1812. Battle of Chippewa (5 July): American defeat of British
force; Battle of Lundy's Lane (25 July): American attempt to take
British position failed; The White House and the Capitol in
Washington burned by British troops (24 August); Battle of Lake
Champlain (11 September): British fleet defeated by Americans;
British launched first of several unsuccessful attacks on New
Orleans, unaware of peace agreement (December); Treaty of Ghent
(signed 24 December) ended the war.

Malta annexed to Britain under the terms of the Treaty of Paris; Cape
Province, South Africa, bought by Britain; Rodrigues ceded to
Britain by Portugal; St Lucia and Seychelles ceded to Britain by
France.

Opening of the Congress of Vienna (1 October, lasted until 9 June
1915).

Gurkha War. Siege of Kalunga (October): Gurkha fort taken by
British troops.

Publication of Sir Walter Scott's *Waverley*.

Early locomotive constructed by George Stephenson.

Present ground of the Marylebone Cricket Club opened. First
matched played there 22 June.

1815

First of the Corn Laws passed in Britain and in 1828 and 1842
(repealed 1844 and 1869).

Gurkha War. Battle of Jitgurh (14 January): Gurkhas defeated British
troops; Battle of Almorah (25 April): British victory over Gurkhas.

War of 1812. Last attack on New Orleans by British, unaware of
peace agreement (8 January): defeated by Americans under Andrew
Jackson.

Napoleon landed in France (March 5): the Hundred Days began;
Battle of Quatre-Bras (16 June) between the British and the French:
Wellington defeated Ney (June 16); Battle of Ligny (16 June):
Blucher defeated after hard fight; Battle of Waterloo (18 June):
Napoleon defeated by Wellington and Blucher; abdication of
Napoleon (June 22); Napoleon surrendered to the British (July 15)
and exiled to St Helena; Treaty of Paris (November): Concert of
Europe established between Britain, Russia, Prussia and Austria.

Introduction into Britain of the quadrille dance.

Invention of the safety lamp for miners by Sir Humphry Davy.
Death of Emma Hamilton, mistress of Lord Nelson (15 January).

1816

Annexation of Tristan da Cunha (settled 1810) by Britain (14 August).

Gurkha War. Battle of Mukwanpur (27 February): attack by Gurkha forces repelled by British with heavy losses.

Bombardment of Algiers by British ships to halt slavery.

Luddite anti-machinery riots.

Radical meeting at Spa Fields broken up.

First portable fire extinguisher invented by George Manby, a barrack-master.

Macadamized roads invented by John Macadam.

The kaleidoscope invented by David Brewster.

Death of the playwright Richard Brinsley Sheridan (7 July).

c.1816

Whigs used name of Liberal Party (adopted officially in 1830s).

1817

Death of Princess Charlotte, daughter of George IV and wife of Leopold of Saxe-Coburg.

Seditious Meetings Act in Britain passed by Castlereagh, suspending Habeas Corpus Act.

Third Maratha War. Battle of Kirkee (5 November): Marathas under Baji Rao defeated by Colonel Burr; Battle of Sitabaldi (24 November): attack by the rajah of Nagpur withstood by British-led troops; Battle of Mahidpur (21 December): British defeat of the Marathas.

Acquittal of the publisher William Hone: important development in the freedom of the press.

Publication of Ricardo's *Principles of Political Economy.*

Blackwood's Magazine founded in Edinburgh.

Kalium (potassium) discovered by Sir Humphrey Davy.

Deaths: Jane Austen (18 July); Captain Bligh (7 December).

1818

Third Maratha War. Battle of Korygaom (1 January): Maratha attack on British defeated; Battle of Ashtee (18 February): rout of Maratha army; Siege of Asirghar begun by British (18 March), garrison

surrendered (7 April); Siege of Chanda (9–11 May): British troops
took Maratha fortress; Battle of Sholapur (10 May): Peshwa's army
finally defeated. End of last Maratha War in India; Maratha power
completely destroyed.

Congress of Aix-la-Chapelle: France admitted to the Concert of Europe.

Institution of Civil Engineers founded (granted Royal Charter 1828).

Completion by Mary Wollstonecraft Shelley of the novel
   Frankenstein (begun 1816).

Publication of *Family Shakespeare* by Bowdler.

Soporific properties of ether discovered by Faraday (first used as an
   anaesthetic 1846).

1819

Birth of a daughter (later Queen Victoria) to the Duke of Kent and
   Princess Mary Louisa Victoria of Saxe-Coburg-Gotha (24 May).

The Six Acts in Britain restricting right of meeting, etc.

Foundation of Singapore by Stamford Raffles.

Burlington Arcade, London, opened (20 March).

Peterloo Massacre at reform meeting near Manchester (16 August):
   eleven killed by soldiers dispersing the meeting.

Radical meeting at Bonnymuir dispersed.

First crossing of the Atlantic by a steam-powered ship, the *Savannah*
   (24 May–20 June).

First rubber factory built in London by Thomas Hancock, who
   patented the vulcanization of rubber.

Cash payments resumed in Britain.

Death of James Watt (19 August).

1820

Cato Street Conspiracy to assassinate the members of the Cabinet
   discovered (23 February): the leader, Arthur Thistlewood, and four
   others executed.

Death of George III (29 January). The Prince Regent became king of
   Britain as George IV.

Failure of George IV's Divorce Bill. He was unable to divorce Caroline.

First British settlers in South Africa (10 April).

Congress of Troppau: Britain and France dissented from the reaction-
   ary protocol.

Foundation of the Royal Astronomical Society (chartered 1831).

1821

Coronation of George IV (19 July): Queen Caroline was barred from attending.

Death of Queen Caroline.

Foundation of the *Manchester Guardian* (named changed to *The Guardian* 1959).

Discovery of plesiosaurus remains by Mary Anning.

Death of John Keats from tuberculosis in Rome (23 February).

1822

Suicide of Lord Castlereagh: Canning succeeded him.

Hetton railway line, Co. Durham, first mineral railway in Britain and first railway on a prepared surface (built by George Stephenson) opened.

Death by drowning in Italy of Shelley (8 July).

1823

Birkbeck College, London University, founded (as the London Mechanics' Institution) by Dr George Birkbeck.

Foundation of the Royal Society of British Artists.

Foundation of *The Lancet* medical journal by Thomas Wakley.

Invention of the waterproof coat by Charles Macintosh.

The dynamo invented by William Sturgeon.

Establishment of the Baltic Exchange in London.

Rugby football began to be played at Rugby School (legalized 1846).

Death of Edward Jenner (26 January).

1824

Laws against combinations repealed in Britain (and in 1825). Trade unions became legal.

First Ashanti War. First Battle of Accra: Ashanti victory over British troops.

First Burma War. British forces took Burmese positions at Kemendine (10 June), Kamarut (8 July) and Kokein (12 December).

Portuguese settlement of Malacca came under British rule.

Athenaeum Club founded in London.

Foundation of the Royal Society for the Prevention of Cruelty to Animals.

Foundation of the Royal Naval Lifeboat Institution by Sir William Hillary (4 March).

Foundation of the National Gallery in London.
Westminster Review started: organ of Radicals.
Imperial standard measure of the gallon legalized.
Portland cement patented by Joseph Aspdin (21 October).
Death from fever of Lord Byron in Greece, fighting for Greek
  independence from Turkey (19 April).

1825

Financial crisis in Britain.
First Ashanti War. Second Battle of Accra: British victory over Ashanti.
First Burma War. Battle of Donabew (7–25 March): British seized
  Burmese stockades; Battle of Watigaon (15 November): British
  attack on Burmese failed; Battle of Pagahar: British defeated Burmese.
Actinometer invented by Sir John Herschel.
Electromagnet invented by William Sturgeon.
Opening of the Stockton and Darlington Railway, the first public
  steam railway (27 September).
Navigation Laws partly repealed.

1826

First Ashanti War. Ashanti invasion of Gold Coast. Battle of
  Dodowah: Ashanti defeated by British.
Straits Settlements of Malaya formed from Penang, Wellesley,
  Malacca and Singapore.
Protocol of St Petersburg regarding Greece: between Britain and
  Russia; end of defence of Missolonghi.
Burke's Peerage founded by Sir John Burke.
Completion of Menai suspension bridge (begun 1818) by Thomas
  Telford.
Foundation of the Zoological Society in London by Sir Stamford Raffles.
Invention of the reaper by Patrick Bell.

1827

Canning became prime minister: Whig coalition. Death of Canning (8
  August): Goderich became prime minister.
Foundation of Ottawa, Canada, (as Bytown) by John By.
Greek War of Independence. Battle of Navarino between the Allied
  and Egyptian fleets (20 October): Treaty of London regarding
  Greece: between Britain, Russia, and France (6 July). Turkish fleet
  destroyed by Allied fleet under Codrington.

Publication of *Shepherd 's Calendar* by John Clare.

The Evening Standard newspaper founded (asborbed the *St James's Gazette* 1905).

Bright's disease identified by Dr Richard Bright.

Charles Babbage began work on his 'analytical engine', the prototype for modern computers (completed 1847).

First suggestion of feasibility of contact lenses by Sir John Herschel (first made in Germany in 1887).

Wooden friction matches invented by John Walker.

Death of William Blake (12 August).

1828

Repeal of Test and Corporation Acts.

Wellington became prime minister (26 January, until 1830).

O'Connell elected for Clare.

Foundation of London University (chartered 1836). Opening of University College, London University.

Opening of Regent's Park, London (27 April).

Thomas Arnold became headmaster of Rugby.

Athenaeum periodical began publication (absorbed into *The Nation* 1921).

Foundation of *The Spectator* (second) by Robert Rintoul.

Brownian Motion in physics discovered by Robert Brown.

Invention of the Nicol prism for the polarization of light by William Nicol.

Marble Arch built.

Darling River in Australia discovered by Charles Sturt.

1829

Catholic Emancipation Act passed in Britain (April); Catholics allowed access to Parliament.

Final repeal of the Test Act.

Functions of the Bow Street Runners superseded by the setting up of the Metropolitan Police Force by Peel as Home Secretary (19 June).

The practice of suttee made illegal in India.

Foundation of King's College, London University.

The Catholic Apostolic Church (or Irvingites) sect founded by Edward Irving.

Concertina invented.

Completion of St Katharine's Dock, Port of London, by Thomas Telford.

First scheduled omnibus service in London (4 July, from Marylebone Road to the Bank).

The manufacture of steel pen nibs perfected by Josiah Mason and Joseph Gillot.

The Rainhill locomotive trials (6 October): victory of George and Robert Stephenson's 'Rocket', the first successful high-speed locomotive.

Oxford and Cambridge Boat Race first held (10 June).

Death of Sir Humphry Davy at Geneva (29 May).

1830

Death of George IV (26 June). His brother became king of Britain as William IV.

Death of William Huskisson, former President of the Board of Trade, by being run over by a train at the opening of the Manchester-Liverpool railway (15 September).

Wellington succeeded by Earl Grey as prime minister (until 1834).

Conference of London recognized Belgian independence.

Foundation of the Plymouth Brethern religious sect by the Rev. John Darby.

Royal Geographical Society founded by Sir John Barrow.

The principles of induction discovered by Michael Faraday.

c.1830

First prefabricated house built as a toll house on the West Bromwich to Birmingham road (dismantled 1926).

1831

Second Reading of first Reform Bill carried in House of Commons by majority of 1 (March 21); hostile amendment carried (April); Parliament dissolved (April 22); majority for Reform elected.

House of Lords rejected first Reform Bill in its second form (8 October).

Truck Act passed, prohibiting payment in kind.

British Guiana in northeast South America became a British colony.

British Association for the Advancement of Science founded.

Opening of second London Bridge, designed by John Rennie (1 August, begun 1824).

Hackney carriages regularized by the Carriage Act.

The laws of electromagnetic induction defined by Faraday.

HMS *Beagle* began five-year scientific circumnavigation of the world with Charles Darwin aboard (27 December).

Enderby Land, Antarctica, discovered by John Biscoe.

King William Island, Arctic, discovered by James Clark Ross.

North magnetic pole located by James Clark Ross.

1832

British Cabinet recommended creation of peers to pass Reform Bill: King William IV refused: Wellington failed to form a ministry: king then agreed: Lords passed the Bill. First Reform Bill became law (4 June) and greatly increased electoral franchise.

Dod's *Parliamentary Companion* founded by Charles Dod.

General election: Whig triumph.

Establishment of shore stations in Otago, New Zealand.

Book jackets first used in England (in general used by 1890).

Durham University founded.

Electroplating invented by George Elkington.

Deaths: Jeremy Bentham; Sir Walter Scott (21 September).

1833

Factory Act forbade employment of children below the age of nine.

Act for Emancipation of British colonial slaves.

Election of the first Quaker MP.

Falkland Islands claimed by Britain as a Crown Colony.

Launch of the Oxford Movement by John Keble (14 July).

Sartor Resartus by Thomas Carlyle.

Electrolysis investigated by Michael Faraday.

Deaths: the philanthropist William Wilberforce (29 July); the civil engineer Thomas Telford (2 September).

1834

Abolition of slavery in British possessions.

Lord Grey resigned: Lord Melbourne became prime minister.

Poor Law Act in England reformed Poor Law system. Introduction of workhouses.

William IV dismissed Melbourne and summoned Peel.

The island of St Helena became a British Crown Colony.

Tolpuddle Martyrs transported for trade union activity.

End of the practice of burying suicides at crossroads, transfixed by a stake.
Palace of Westminster destroyed by fire except Westminster Hall and St Stephen's Chapel (16 October).
The Veto Act passed by the Scottish General Assembly.
The hansom cab patented by Joseph Hansom (23 December).
Deaths: the poet Samuel Taylor Coleridge (25 July); the essayist Charles Lamb (27 December).

1835

Municipal Reform Act.
Peel resigned: Melbourne recalled (in office until 1841).
Sir George Airy made Astronomer Royal.
Foundation of Madame Tussaud's Waxworks in London by Mme Marie Tussaud.
Appearance of Halley's Comet (named after Edmund Halley).
Cuneiform writing first deciphered by Sir Henry Rawlinson.
Electric telegraph invented.
First surviving photograph taken by William Fox Talbot.
Bear-baiting and bull-baiting prohibited by Act of Parliament.

1836

Beginning of Chartist movement (ended c.1858).
Adelaide, South Australia founded (named after Queen Adelaide).
Beginning of the Great Trek of Boers in South Africa, from Cape Colony to the Orange Free State. Transvaal first colonized by Boers.
Tolpuddle Martyrs pardoned.
Non-religious marriages made legal.
Orange Lodges dissolved.
Acetylene discovered by Edmund Davy.
Appointment of the first Registrar-General, Thomas Lister.
Invention of the screw propeller by Francis Pettit Smith.

1837

Death of William IV (20 June). His niece Victoria became queen of Britain.
French-Canadian Rebellion in Canada under Papineau and Mackenzie; rebels victorious at Battle of St Denis, but defeated at the Battles of St Charles and St Eustache.
Indian Post Office established (24 July).

The registration of births, marriages and deaths made compulsory in England and Wales (1 July).

Publication completed of *The Posthumous Papers of the Pickwick Club* by Charles Dickens (begun 1836): his first novel.

Opening of Euston Railway Station, first in London (20 July).

Discovery of the polarization of heat by James Forbes.

Invention of the railway ticket dating machine by Thomas Edmondson.

Publication of *Stenographic Sound Hand* by Isaac Pitman, demonstrating Pitman's shorthand (15 November).

The first practical telegraph line patented by William Cooke and Charles Wheatstone.

The invention of penny postage by Rowland Hill (who put it into effect in 1840).

Grand National horse race first run at Liverpool.

Death of the artist John Constable (31 March).

1838

Act of Parliament brought the Public Records under the superintendence of the Master of the Rolls.

Anti-Corn Law League founded by Richard Cobden and John Bright.

People's Charter published.

Afrikaner-Zulu War. Massacre of Boers by Zulu chief Dingaan. Battle of Dingaan's Day (16 December): Boer revenge on Zulus.

Lord Durham became governor-general of Canada.

Grace Darling resued survivors of the *Forfarshire* (7 September).

Foundation of the Peculiar People religious movement in London.

Opening of the National Gallery in London (9 April).

Invention of the bicycle by Kirkpatrick Macmillan.

*c.*1838

Invention of the stereoscope by Charles Wheatstone.

1839

Peel became prime minister: resigned on Bedchamber question when Victoria rejected the proposal that some of her Whig Ladies of the Bedchamber be replaced by Conservatives: Melbourne resumed office.

Petition by Chartist movement rejected by Parliament (also in 1842 and 1848).

Rebecca Riots in Wales destroyed tollhouses and tollgates.

Aden annexed to British India.

Durham's Report on Canada submitted to British Parliament.

First Afghan War began (ended 1842). Khelat captured by British (13 November).

Treaty of London: final adjustment of Belgian frontiers and recognition by Holland.

Indian tea reached Britain for the first time.

First publication of *Bradshaw's Railway Guide* (Great Britain) by George Bradshaw (25 October, discontinued 1961).

Invention of the steam hammer by James Nasmyth.

The Grove cell electric battery invented by William Grove.

Cunard steampship company founded (4 May).

Cesarewitch Stakes, Newmarket, first run.

Grand National first run at Aintree (26 February).

First Henley Regatta at Henley-on-Thames held (14 June).

1840

O'Connell revived the Repeal Association.

Marriage of Queen Victoria and Prince Albert of Saxe-Coburg (10 February).

End of convict transportation to New South Wales.

Treaty of Waitangi between Captain Hobson and Maori chiefs in New Zealand (6 February); New Zealand proclaimed a British colony (21 May).

Union Act for Canada: responsible government granted: an epoch in colonial history.

Beirut bombarded by Sir Charles Napier.

Convention of London: Four Powers to Act against Mehemet Ali in Egypt: France stood aloof; British and Turkish troops attacked and destroyed Acre; Egyptians defeated.

Outbreak of the Opium War between Britain and China on opium question (ended 1842).

Penny postage introduced in Britain by its inventor, Rowland Hill (10 January); Adhesive postage stamps first used (6 May); stamped envelopes issued.

Livingstone began his work in Africa.

London Library founded (opened 1841).

Introduction of the term 'scientist' by William Whewell, Master of
   Trinity College, Cambridge.
Lake Eyre, South Australia, discovered by Edward Eyre.

1841

Birth of a son, Albert Edward (later Edward VII), to Queen Victoria
   and Prince Albert (9 November); created Prince of Wales (8
   December).
Melbourne, defeated after a dissolution, resigned: Peel became prime
   minister (until 1845).
Richard Moody made first governor of the Falkland Islands (until
   1849).
Foundation of Thomas Cook's, travel agents, by Thomas Cook.
First publication of *Punch* (17 July) by Ebenezer Landells and Mark
   Lemon.
Completion of construction (began 1811) of Plymouth breakwater,
   designed by John Rennie.
Foundation of the Pharmaceutical Society of Great Britain (incorpo-
   ration by Royal Charter 1843).
Joule's Law of electrical energy pronounced by James Joule.
Standardization of screw threads by Joseph Whitworth.
The term 'hypnotism' first introduced by James Braid.
Mount Erebus, volcanic mountain in Antarctica, discovered by Sir
   James Clark Ross.

1842

Assam conquered by the British.
First Afghan War. British army evacuating Kabul attacked at Khoord
   Kabul Pass (8 January) and at Jugdulluk (12 January); Siege of
   British at Jellalabad began (11 March); British defeated at Khojah
   Pass (28 March); Battle of Maidan (14 September): Afghans
   defeated.
Treaty of Nanking (29 August): end of the Opium War. Hong Kong
   leased to Britain by China (20 January); New Territories, Kowloon
   and Stonecutters Island added 1898.
Claim of Right by Scottish Church.
Foundation of Mudie's Library (existed until 1937) by Charles Mudie.
The *Illustrated London News* began publication (14 May).
The Nation began in Dublin.

Blueprint process for copying plans, etc, first used by Sir John
  Herschel.
King Edward VII Land, Antarctica, sighted by James Clark Ross.

1843

Sind Conquest. Battle of Miani (17 February): hard-fought British
  defeat of Beluchi forces. Battle of Dubba (24 March): British
  defeated Beluchi forces. Battle of Hyderabad (24 August): Beluchis
  defeated; Napier's conquest of Sind complete.
First Afghan War. Relief of British at Jellalabad (18 April).
Gwalior Campaign. Battle of Maharajpur (29 December): British
  victory.
Natal declared British.
The Gambia made an independent British Crown Colony.
Entente cordiale between France and Britain.
First International Peace Congress held in London.
Khaki first worn by the Queen's Own Corps of Scouts and Guides
  (became general in second Afghan War).
Rebecca Riots in Wales.
First Christmas cards produced in Britain.
The MacNaghten Rules formulated as the legal definition of insanity
  after the trial for murder of Daniel MacNaghten.
Foundation of the Evangelical Union by James Morison.
Free Church founded in Scotland by the Disruption: Dr Thomas
  Chalmers the leader.
William Wordsworth became poet laureate (6 April) after the death of
  Robert Southey (21 March).
The Economist magazine founded by James Wilson.
First publication of the *News of the World* (1 October).
Building of the first ocean-going iron ship (the *Great Britain*) by
  Isambard Kingdom Brunel; launched by Prince Albert 19 July.
Opening of the Thames Tunnel (begun 1825), the world's first
  underwater tunnel, built by Sir Marc Isambard Brunel, still in use
  by London Underground (25 March).
Foundation of the Royal College of Surgeons in London (21 June).
Foundation of the world's first agricultural experimental station at
  Rothamsted by John Lawes.
Hydroelectricity discovered by Michael Faraday.

Patent granted to Thomas Hancock for the vulcanization of rubber (21 November).

The Royal Hunt Cup horse race first ran at Ascot.

1844

Railway Act. Bank Charter Act.

Annexation of Natal to Cape Colony.

Fleet Prison pulled down.

Foundation of the YMCA (Young Men's Christian Association) by George Williams.

First co-operative store opened by the Rochdale Society (21 December): origin of Co-operative Societies.

Establishment of the Imperial standard weight of the pound and standard measure of the yard.

Death of the scientist John Dalton (27 July).

1845

Peel forced to resign.Lord John Russell failed to form a ministry.

First Sikh War. Battle of Mudki (18 December): failure of Sikh attack on British troops; Battle of Ferozeshah (21 December): bloody draw between the British and Sikhs.

Failure of the potato crop (until 1849): great distress in Ireland, etc.

Portland Vase deliberately destroyed in the British Museum (7 February).

Experiments on the polarization of light made by Michael Faraday.

Invention of the Moon alphabet for the blind by Dr William Moon.

The pneumatic tyre was patented by Robert Thomson (10 December).

Position of the planet Neptune predicted by John Couch Adams.

The *Great Britain* set out from Liverpool on her maiden voyage, to New York (26 July).

Death of the prison reformer Elizabeth Fry (12 October).

c.1845

Hydraulic crane invented by William Armstrong.

Tonic sol-fa system invented by Sarah Glover.

1846

Repeal of the Corn Laws.

Defeat and resignation of Peel: Russell formed a ministry (until 1852).

First Sikh War. Battle of Aliwal (28 January): British victory over the

Sikhs; Battle of Sobraon (10 February): British defeated Sikhs. End of war.

Kashmir recognized British supremacy.

Entente cordiale between Britain and France broken off on question of Spanish marriages.

Foundation of Manchester University (as Owens College) by John Owens.

Foundation of Secularism by George Holyoake.

Marriage of Robert Browning and Elizabeth Barrett.

Publication of *Book of Nonsense* by Edward Lear.

The Daily News newspaper founded (merged in *News Chronicle* 1930).

1847

Ten Hours Act in Britain.

Lord Elgin became governor-general of Canada (until 1854): made responsible government a reality.

Foundation of the Oratory, Birmingham.

Excavation completed (began 1845) of Nineveh, the Assyrian capital, by Sir Austen Layard.

Publication of *Jane Eyre* by Charlotte Brontë, *Wuthering Heights* by Emily Brontë and *Agnes Grey* by Anne Brontë.

Publication of *Vanity Fair* by Thackeray.

Chloroform first used as an anaesthetic.

James 'Paraffin' Young began experimenting with the distillation of oil distilled from coal and shale (completed 1850).

Deaths: Daniel O'Connell (15 May); the explorer Sir John Franklin while attempting to discover the Northwest Passage (11 June).

1848

Transportation of leaders of Young Ireland.

Battle of Boomplaatz (29 August): Boers defeated by Sir Harry Smith, governor of the Cape of Good Hope. Orange Free State proclaimed British Territory.

Dalhousie made governor-general of India (until 1856).

First officially organized settlement in Otago, New Zealand.

Second Sikh War. outbreak in India (ended 1849) between the British and the Sikhs: Punjab annexed. Battle of Kineyri (18 June): Sikhs defeated and fled to Multan; Battle of Suddasain (1 July): Sikh attack on British-led forces defeated; Siege of Multan began (July).

Chartist demonstration in London a fiasco.

Publication of *The Communist Manifesto* by Karl Marx.

John Bird Sumner became archbishop of Canterbury (until 1862).

Continental *Bradshaw* established.

Deaths: George Stephenson (12 August); Lord Melbourne (24
   November); Emily Brontë (19 December).

1849

Second Sikh War. Multan stormed (2 January) and surrendered (22
   January); Battle of Chilianwala (14 January): British and Indian
   troops under Lord Gough defeated the Sikhs; Battle of Gujerat (22
   February): British and Indian troops under Gough crushed the
   Sikhs; Battle of Ramnuggur (22 November): British attempt to
   dislodge Sikh army unsuccessful.

Complete repeal of Navigation Laws in Britain (and 1854).

Cockfighting made illegal.

Foundation of the Royal London Homeopathic Hospital by Dr
   Frederick Quin.

Deaths: Anne Brontë (28 May); Queen Adelaide, widow of William
   IV (2 December).

1850

First British Public Library Act passed (superseded by the Act of
   1919), permitting the establishment of public libraries in England.

Foundation of the Meteorological Office in London by James
   Glaisher.

Opening of the first reformatory in Britain at Redhill.

The Koh-i-Noor diamond presented to the British regalia by the East
   India Company.

Christian Socialism founded by John Ludlau.

Publication of Tennyson's *In Memoriam.*

Death of the poet laureate William Wordsworth (23 April). Lord
   Tennyson appointed poet laureate (19 November).

Collodion process invented by Frederick Archer.

Discovery of the spiral nebulae announced by the Earl of Rosse.

Initiation of synthetic oil production by James 'Paraffin' Young.

Process of mercerising invented by John Mercer.

The hydraulic pressure accumulator invented by William Armstrong.

Death of Sir Robert Peel following a riding accident (2 July).

*c.*1850

First kindergarten in England opened.

1851

Palmerston dismised from Foreign Office for unauthorized recognition of the French coup d'état.

Catholic hierarchy restored in Britain and Holland.

The Great Exhibition in London (1 May-15 October) held in the Crystal Palace (designed by Joseph Paxton), Hyde Park, London.

Publication of cheap editions of music pioneered by Henry Litolff.

Publication of *Lavengro* by George Borrow.

Development of the mathematical theory of determinants by William Spottiswoode.

Discovery of the organic base pyridine by Thomas Anderson.

First telegraph cable laid across the English Channel.

Invention of instantaneous photography by William Fox Talbot.

Marble Arch (built 1828) re-erected at Cumberland Gate, Hyde Park.

The first envelope-making machine invented by Warren de la Rue.

Gold found in the Blue Hills, New South Wales, Australia, leading to a gold rush (February).

Deaths: the writer Mary Shelley (1 February); the painter Joseph Turner.

1852

Coalition government. Fall of Derby ministry. Russell defeated: Derby became prime minister.

Annexation of Lower Burma by Britain.

Signature of the Sand River Convention (17 January): Britain recognized independence of Transvaal.

Great Ormond Street Hospital for children opened for patients (14 February).

Last duel fought in England at Priest Hill, Surrey.

Compilation of *Roget's Thesaurus* by Peter Mark Roget.

Opening of the Victoria and Albert Museum in London.

Invention of quaternions vector analysis by William Hamilton.

Alpaca fabrics first manufactured in England by Sir Titus Salt.

Death of the Duke of Wellington (14 September).

1853

Aberdeen coalition ministry with Earl of Aberdeen as prime minister.

Orange River Sovereignty abandoned by Britain.

Abolition of soap tax (imposition 1712).

Chetham's Library, Manchester, founded by Humfrey Chetham.

Newspaper advertisement duty abolished.

The troy ounce measure for precious metals legalized in Britain.

David Livingstone discovered the Victoria Falls.

1854

Ecclesiastical Titles Bill in Britain: abortive.

Orange Free State established as independent.

British and French troops occupied the Piraeus.

Crimean War. British and French troops landed in the Crimea; the
Allies (Britain, Turkey and France) and Russia (ended 1856); Battle
of the Alma (20 September): Russians defeated; Siege of Sebastopol
began (28 September); Battle of Balaklava (25 October) between
the Russians and the British the outcome of which was indecisive:
Charge of the Light Brigade; Battle of Inkerman between the
Russians and British (5 November): Russians defeated.

Cigarettes introduced into Britain.

Crystal Palace moved to Penge.

Institute of Chartered Accountants of Scotland chartered.

Voyage of discovery of the Northwest Passage completed (began
1850) by Robert McClure.

1855

Aberdeen defeated and resigned: Palmerston became prime minister.

Suppression of Donnybrook Fair in Ireland.

Crimean War. Sardinia joined Britain and France in Crimean War;
death of Lord Raglan (28 June); Battle of the Great Redan (8
September): unsuccessful British attack on southern defences of
Sebastopol; Siege of Sebastopol ended with seizure (9 September).

Letters of Marque, granted to allow private persons to fit out armed
ships in wartime, abolished by the Declaration of Paris.

Building of Balmoral Castle completed.

Jews' College, London, founded by Nathan Adler, Chief Rabbi.

Last Bartholomew Fair held at West Smithfield London on St
Bartholomew's Day (began 1133).

The registration of births, marriages and deaths made compulsory in
Scotland.

Newspaper stamp tax abolished.

The Daily Telegraph newspaper refounded by Joseph Moses Levy (29 June).

Addison's disease discovered by Thomas Addison.

Cellulose nitrate, first synthetic plastic material, invented by Alexander Parkes.

  Celluloid patented by Alexander Parkes.

The study of astrophysics founded by Sir William Huggins.

Creation of the first registered trademark, the Red Badge of Bass & Co.'s Pale Ale.

Death of Charlotte Brontë (31 March).

1856

Annexation of Oude to British India.

British Guiana issued the most valuable postage stamp (only one copy known) in February.

Natal made a British colony.

Norfolk Island in the South Pacific settled (became an external territory of Australia 1913).

Crimean War: ended by signature of the Treaty of Paris (30 March).

Foundation by Queen Victoria of the Victoria Cross, the premier decoration for valour (29 January), made from the iron of Russian cannon used by the Russians at Sebastopol.

Elizabeth Garrett Anderson qualified as first British woman doctor.

Publication of *Tom Brown's Schooldays* by Thomas Hughes.

Anilines dyes discovered by William Henry Perkin.

Bessemer converter invented by Henry Bessemer.

Origination of the paraffin industry by James 'Paraffin' Young.

1857

Prince Albert created Prince Consort.

Bank Charter Act suspended.

Lord Canning became governor-general of India. Indian Mutiny. Outbreak at Meerut when troops who had objected to biting off the ends of cartridges greased with animal fat were court-martialled (10 May); Massacre of Cawnpore (6 June): members of the English garrison and their families murdered by rioters; Jhansi captured by mutineers (June); Residency at Lucknow defended by the Duke of Cornwall's Light Infantry (1 July); Mutineers defeated by British force advancing on Cawnpore at Aong and Pandu Naddi (15 July);

Defeat of rebels at Maharajpur (16 July) and Onao (28 July); Battle of Agra (2 August): British garrison forced back into the fort; Battle of Nujufghur (24 August) rebels defeated by British force; Battle of Agra (October): British force put rebels to flight. Sir Henry Havelock's relief of Lucknow began (19 September). Delhi besieged by British (from 8 June); palace taken (20 September). Battle of Secunderbagh (16 November): rebel stronghold stormed by British and Indian troops. Campbell relieved garrison at Lucknow (19 November). Mutineers defeated at Goraria (23–24 November) and Pandu Naddi (26 November). Battle of Cawnpore (6 December): British under Sir Colin Campbell routed the mutineers.

Arrow incident in China led to war: Palmerston defeated in Parliament: appealed to the country and obtained a majority.

Britannia Royal Naval College founded at Portland (transferred to Dartmouth 1863).

International Code of Signals devised by the British government (amended 1901).

Merger as the United Methodists of a group of Methodist sects (added to in 1907).

Foundation of the National Portrait Gallery (opened 1859).

Publication of *Barchester Towers* by Anthony Trollope.

The Halle Orchestra in Manchester established by Sir Charles Halle.

First telegraph cable laid across the Atlantic.

1858

Palmerston defeated on Orsini question: Derby Premier.

The Fenians (Irish Republican Brotherhood), an Irish-American revolutionary movement founded in the USA.

The Jewish Disabilities Removal Act passed, allowing Jewish members of the House of Commons (to the House of Lords 1885).

British Columbia constituted a British Crown Colony (2 August).

Indian Mutiny. Mutineer-held palace of Musa Bagh at Lucknow captured by British (19 March); Relief of the city of Lucknow finally achieved (21 March); Mutineers besieged at Kotah (22 March) and captured (30 March) by Lord Roberts; Jhansi recaptured by British (2 April); Battle of Azimghur (15 April): British and Sikh troops defeated rebels; British besieged and captured Kalpi (19–23 May); Battle of Baduli-ki-Serai (8 June): mutineers defeated by

British force; Battle of Gwalior (17–19 June): Sir Hugh Rose
  defeated mutineers.

Government of India transferred to the Crown: title of viceroy
  implemented; Lord Canning became first viceroy; East India
  Company dissolved.

Big Ben hour bell cast (10 April).

First regular public concert by the Halle Orchestra (30 January).

Opening of Covent Garden Theatre (now the Royal Opera House) in
  London (15 May).

Bishop Rock Lighthouse completed.

First Atlantic cable completed (5 August).

First meeting of the General Medical Council held (23 November).

Geologists' Association founded (17 December).

Launch of the *Great Eastern*, designed by Isambard Kingdom Brunel
  (31 January).

London divided into postal districts.

The Darwin's theory of evolution by natural selection first read to the
  Linnean Society of London (1 July).

Discovery of Lake Victoria by John Speke (3 August).

Discovery of Lake Tanganyika by Burton and Speke.

Deaths: the engineer Robert Stephenson (12 October); the social
  reformer Robert Owen (17 November).

*c.*1858

Steel rails first made by the industrialist John Brown.

1859

Lord Palmerston again prime minister (until 1865).

Formation of Queensland, Australia, into a separate colony.

London Irish Volunteer Rifles formed (25 November).

Volunteer movement arose in Britain: the Royal Naval Reserve
  (Volunteers) Act led to the formation of the Royal Naval Reserve.

Big Ben into service (31 May).

Closure of Vauxhall Gardens in London (opened *c.*1661).

Corps of Commissionaires founded by Sir Edward Walter for
  employment of ex-soldiers (13 February).

Dr Elizabeth Blackwell became first British registered woman doctor.

The district nursing movement introduced in Britain by William
  Rathbone.

First Cruft's dog show held in Newcastle.

Chambers's Encyclopaedia founded by William Chambers (completed 1868).

First publication of Darwin's *Origin of Species*, *On Liberty* by John Stuart Mill, Meredith's *Ordeal of Richard Feverel* and *The Rubaiyat of Omar Khayyam* by Edward FitzGerald.

The kinetic theory of gases postulated by James Clerk Maxwell.

Lake Nyasa (now Lake Malawi) discovered by David Livingstone.

Death of the engineer Isambard Kingdom Brunel (15 September).

1860

Lords rejected repeal of paper duties: Gladstone overcame their opposition.

Maori Wars began in New Zealand (ended 1870).

Commercial Treaty between Britain and France negotiated by Richard Cobden.

Treaty of Tientsin ended war in China: more ports opened.

Launch of HMS *Warrior*, the first British iron-clad warship (29 December).

Aberdeen University formed by the amalgamation of King's College and Marischal College.

Foundation by Florence Nightingale of the first British training school for nurses at St Thomas's Hospital, London.

Ruskin completed *Modern Painters*.

First transportation by sea of petroleum from the USA to Europe arrived in London.

Foundation of the Institution of Naval Architects.

Introduction of trams into England, at Birkenhead (30 August).

Linoleum invented by Frederick Walton.

An incandescent electric lamp invented by Swan.

Centre of Australia first reached by John McDouall Stuart.

Last bare-knuckle prize fight held in England (17 April).

1861

Death of Prince Albert, the Prince Consort, from typhoid (14 December.

Bahrain became British protectorate.

Debate at Oxford University on Darwin's theory of natural selection between Thomas Huxley ('Darwin's Bulldog', for) and Bishop Wilberforce (against).

Introduction of the Post Office Savings Bank (16 September).

Completion of publication (began 1849) of Lord Macaulay's *History of England*.

Publication of *The Golden Treasury* anthology by Palgrave.

Discovery of the metallic element thallium by William Crookes.

Invention by Joseph Reade of Reade's kettledrum, a condenser for the microscope.

The study of colloidal chemistry initiated by Thomas Graham.

Gold found in the Otago, New Zealand.

First British Golf Open championship held at Prestwick (26 September).

Death of the poet Elizabeth Barrett Browning in Florence (30 June).

1862

British Honduras (now Belize) declared a British colony.

Cotton famine in Lancashire.

Land registry established (reformed 1875; now operating under Land Registration Acts 1925-88).

First Lambeth Bridge in London opened.

Speke and Grant discovered sources of the River Nile.

1863

Marriage of the Prince of Wales (later Edward VII) and Princess Alexandra of Denmark (10 March).

Fenian Secret Society founded in Ireland to set up Irish republic.

First Ashanti War began (ended 1864).

Broadmoor criminal lunatic asylum opened (27 May).

Carbolic first used as a disinfectant by Lister.

Opening (10 January) of the first underground railway, the Metropolitan Railway in London between Paddington and Farringdon Street.

English Football Association formed (26 October).

The world's first heavyweight boxing championship held (8 December).

Death of the novelist William Thackeray (24 December).

1864

Café Royal founded in London (bombed 1940).

International Working Men's Association founded in London.

Building of Albert Memorial, Hyde Park, began (completed 1876).

Opening of the Clifton Suspension Bridge, Bristol (8 December).

Cotton's knitting frame invented by William Cotton.

First publication of *British Pharmacopoeia*.

The existence of electromagnetic waves established by James Clerk
   Maxwell.
Lake Albert Nyanza discovered by Sir Samuel Baker.

1865

Birth of a second son (later George V) to the Prince of Wales (later
   Edward VII) and Princess Alexandra (3 June).
Death of Lord Palmerston (18 October). Russell became prime
   minister.
Red Flag Act introduced the first road speed limit (5 July).
Foundation of the Salvation Army by William Booth (2 July).
Publication of *Alice's Adventures in Wonderland* by Lewis Carroll,
   illustrated by Tenniel.
Building began on Blackfriars Bridge, London (completed 1869).
Completion of the metropolitan drainage system in London (began
   1855), carried out by Joseph Bazalgette.
The Matterhorn first climbed by Edward Whymper (13 July).

1866

Russell retired following defeat on his franchise bill (June).
   Gladstone introduced a Reform Bill: the Adullamites helped the
   Conservatives to defeat it: Derby ministry followed Russell's
   resignation.
Habeas Corpus Act suspended in Ireland.
Isle of Man gained home rule.
Jamaica established as a British colony. The Gambia incorporated in
   the West African settlements.
Howard League for Penal Reform founded in memory of John
   Howard.
First Atlantic telegraph cable successfully laid by the SS *Great
   Eastern* (completed 7 September).
Foundation of the Royal Aeronautical Society (as the Aeronautical
   Society of Great Britain; name changed 1919).
Invention of the submarine torpedo by Robert Whitehead.
Last major epidemic of cholera in England.
London Salvage Corps founded.
'Black Friday' in London: financial crisis.

1867

Resignations of ministers because of Disraeli's Reform Bill.

Second Reform Act passed as moulded by the Liberal majority.
  electoral franchise doubled to over two million.
Abyssinian Expedition begun by British troops from India (ended
  1868).
British North America Act (1 July) created Dominion of Canada:
  beginning of federation in the Empire. Nova Scotia and Ontario
  became Provinces.
Fenian (Irish Republican Brotherhood) attacks in London, Manches-
  ter, etc.
Barnardo's Homes founded by Dr Thomas Barnardo.
First Lambeth Conference of Anglican bishops convened.
First operation under antiseptic conditions performed by Lister in
  Glasgow (18 June).
Building of Albert Hall, Kensington, in memory of Prince Albert
  began (completed 1871).
First demonstration of dynamite by Alfred Nobel in Surrey (14 July).
Initiation of the Queensberry Rules for boxing with gloves by Lord
  Queensberry.

1868

Disraeli became prime minister on Derby's retirement: defeated on
  question of disestablishing Irish Church.
General election in Britain: Liberal triumph: Gladstone's first
  ministry (9 December, until 1874).
Formation of the Trades Union Congress (TUC). First Congress held
  2–6 June.
Foundation of St Catherine's Society, Oxford University.
Last public execution held in London (26 May).
Foundation of the Press Association in London (29 June).
First publication of *Whitaker's Almanack* by Joseph Whitaker (10
  December).
Publication of *The Moonstone* by Wilkie Collins.
Development of the theory of radio waves (discovered by Hertz) by
  James Clerk Maxwell.
Helium discovered spectroscopically by Joseph Lockyer.
Invention of photochromolithography by William Griggs.
Opening of the Metropolitan District Railway in London between
  Mansion House and South Kensington.

1869

Government passed the Disestablishment Act to disestablish the
   Church of Ireland.
Annexation of the Nicobar Islands in the Bay of Bengal by Britain.
Red River Rebellion in Canada under Louis Riel began: suppressed
   by Wolseley in 1870.
Archibald Tait became archbishop of Canterbury (until 1882).
Buchan's days weather predictions defined by Alexander Buchan.
First publication of *Nature* periodical edited by Joseph Lockyer.
Foundation of the Metaphysical Society by Sir James Knowles.
Introduction of the term 'agnostic' by Thomas Huxley.
Opening of Girton College, Cambridge, as the College for Women
   (16 October). Acquired present name and site in 1872.
Opening of the Suez Canal (17 November).
Telegraph monopoly given to the Post Office.
The Labour Representation League (one of the forerunners of the
   Labour Party) organized.

1870

Bankruptcy Act: abolished imprisonment for debt.
Education Act for England and Wales: primary education compulsory.
Ending of the Maori Wars in New Zealand (began 1860).
Formation of the Old Catholics religious movement (until 1871).
Home Rule for Ireland League founded by Isaac Butt.
Keble College, Oxford, erected in memor of John Keble.
Manitoba, formerly the Red River Colony, admitted to the Dominion
   of Canada (12 May).
Disestablishment and disendowment of the Church of Ireland.
Institute of Accountants (later Institute of Chartered Accountants) in
   England and Wales founded.
Introduction of the postcard and the halfpenny postage stamp (1
   October).
Foundation of the Red Cross Society in Britain (4 August).
America's Cup first competed for by yachts. American *Magic*
   defeated British *Cambria* (8 August).
Death of Charles Dickens (9 June).

1871

Legal recognition of trade unions in Britain (29 June).

Bank Holiday Act (25 May); first bank holiday held on Whit Monday
   (29 May).
British Columbia became a Province of the Dominion of Canada.
Conference of London modified Treaty of Paris of 1856.
Infantry rank of ensign and cavalry rank of cornet abolished.
Foundation of the Institution of Electrical Engineers (as The Society
   of Telegraph Engineers).
The Tichborne Claimant: beginning of Arthur Orton's claim of the
   Tichborne inheritance.
Institution of the practice of photographing prisoners (2 November).
Abolition of religious tests at Oxford University.
Publication completed of *Encyclopaedia Britannica* (began 1768)
   and *Middlemarch* by George Eliot (began 1870).
Opening of the Royal Albert Hall by Queen Victoria (29 March).
Meeting of Stanley and Livingstone at Ujiji (10 November)..
Foundation of the Rugby Union (26 January).
Death of the astronomer Sir John Herschel (11 May).

1872
Ballot Act passed: made voting by secret ballot compulsory.
Self-government in Cape Colony.
College erected in Aberystwyth.
Education Act for Scotland.
The ship *Mary Celeste* found derelict in the Atlantic (5 December).
C. P. Scott became editor of the *Manchester Guardian* (until 1929).
Unveiling of the Albert Memorial in London (1 July).

1873
Second Ashanti War began (ended 1874).
Foundation of Oxford University Observatory.
Formation of the Scottish Football Association (13 March).
Death of Livingstone in Africa (1 May).
Death of the painter Sir Edwin Landseer (1 October).

*c.*1873
Badminton first played in England.

1874
Disraeli became prime minister after a general election (until 1880).
Fiji became a British colony (until 1970).

Second Ashanti War. Battle of Amoaful (31 January): Ashantis defeated by British forces under Sir Garnet Wolseley; Kumasi captured from Ashanti and Gold Coast established as a British colony.

Leeds University founded (granted university status 1904).

Tichborne Claimant: end of Orton's trial for perjury (he was imprisoned until 1884).

Patronage Act repealed in Scotland.

Invention of the safety bicycle by H. J. Lawson.

1875

Foundation of the Universal Postal Union in Bern (9 October).

Birmingham University founded as Mason College by Sir Josiah Mason.

Mrs Emma Anne Paterson became the first woman to be admitted to the Trade Union Congress.

First intelligible telephone communication made by Bell (5 June).

First observation of the photoelectric property of selenium by Willoughby Smith.

English Channel first swum by Captain Matthew Webb (25 August).

Western Australia first reached overland by Ernest Giles at his third attempt.

1876

Queen Victoria proclaimed Empress of India under the terms of Disraeli's Royal Titles Act.

Disraeli bought Khedive's shares in Suez Canal for Britain. International control began in Egypt.

Bristol University founded as University College (granted Royal Charter 24 May 1909).

Regulation of vivisection established by law.

The British medical profession opened up to women through the efforts of Sophia Jex-Blake.

Telephone patented by Bell.

The Plimsoll Line, devised by Samuel Plimsoll, came into force to establish the limit to which a ship may be loaded.

Manchester November Handicap horse race first run 1876.

1877

Britain annexed Transvaal.

The Indian Empire proclaimed.

Library Association of the United Kingdom established.

New Forest scheduled as a National Park.

Formation of the Ambulance Association (later St John's Ambulance Brigade) by the Red Cross (24 June).

Cleopatra's Needle taken from Egypt to London by Sir Erasmus Wilson.

Foundation of *Truth* magazine.

Publication of *Black Beauty* by Anna Sewell.

Stanley explored the Congo.

First day of first Wimbledon lawn tennis championships (9 July).

1878

Second Afghan War began (ended in 1880); British defeated Aghans guarding the Peiwar Kotal Pass (2 December).

Cyprus placed under British administration by Turkey (12 July).

Dog licences required in Britain by Act of Parliament.

Cleopatra's Needle erected on the Embankment in London (12 September).

*c.*1878

Introduction of the Axminster and Wilton carpet into Britain from USA.

1879

Abolition of outlawry in Britain.

First Zulu War. Battle of Isandhlwana (22 January): overwhelming defeat of British troops and Natal volunteers by Zulus; Battle of Rorke's Drift (22–23 January): Zulu attack defeated; Battle of Inhlobane Mountain (28 March): British attack on Zulus defeated; Battle of Kambula (29 March): Zulu attack on British defeated; Battle of Ulundi (4 July): British defeated Zulus; Cetewayo captured (28 August).

Irish Land League founded by Michael Davitt.

Second Afghan War. Battle of Ahmed Khel: attack on British force repulsed; Battle of Charasiab (6 October): British attack on and defeat of Afghan force.

Dual control in Egypt: Britain and France.

Collapse of the Tay railway bridge carrying the Edinburgh to Dundee train (28 December); ninety people killed.

Foundation of Sheffield University (as Firth College) by Mark Firth.

Foundation of Somerville College, Oxford, in memory of Mary

Somerville, St Anne's College, Oxford, and Lady Margaret Hall, Oxford.

John Henry Newman created a cardinal (converted to Catholicism 1845).

First publication of the *Liverpool Echo* (27 October).

Henry George's *Progress and Poverty*.

Reconstruction of Sadler's Wells Theatre.

Incandescent electric lamp patented by Edison.

Invention of an apparatus for determining the flashpoint of petroleum by Frederick Abel.

1880

Gladstone prime minister (until 1885) after a general election.

Greenwich Mean Time made legal time for Britain.

Captain Boycott, Lord Erne's English land agent in Co. Mayo 'boycotted' (from 24 September).

Revolt of Boers in the Transvaal.

Second Afghan War. Battle of Maiwand (27 July): British defeated; Battle of Kandahar (1 September): British victory under Lord Roberts ended war.

Britain recognized Abdurrahman as Amir of Afghanistan.

Institute of Chartered Accountants chartered.

Publication began of the *St James's Gazette* newspaper (absorbed by the *Evening Standard* 1905).

First telephone directory in Britain issued (15 January).

The volcanic mountain Chimborazo in Ecuador first climbed by Edward Whymper.

Amateur Athletic Association founded.

Death of the novelist George Eliot (22 December).

1881

Introduction of postal orders in Britain (1 January).

Irish Land Act.

First Boer War. Battle of Lang's Neck (28 January): British attack on Boers defeated; Battle of Ingogo (8 February): British attack on Boers defeated; Battle of Majuba Hill (27 February): British defeated by Boers; Transvaal independence recognized.

North Borneo made a British protectorate.

Revolt in Egypt against the British and French over the Suez Canal;

Alexandria bombarded by British fleet and Egyptian forts destroyed (11–12 July).

Revolt of the Mahdi in the Sudan.

Nottingham University opened as University College (achieved university status 1948).

Foundation of *TitBits* periodical by George Newnes.

The Evening News newspaper founded (absorbed *The Star* 1960).

Electric light first used domestically in Britain.

First electric power station in England opened at Goldalming.

Fourth Eddystone Lighthouse completed (begun 1879).

Death of Thomas Carlyle (5 February).

Death of Benjamin Disraeli, Earl of Beaconsfield (19 April). That day named Primrose Day because of Disraeli's fondness for the flower.

1882

St Kitts-Nevis and Anguilla made a British colony (until 1967).

Ireland. Phoenix Park murders in Dublin: the murder of the newly appointed chief secretary for Ireland, Lord Frederick Cavendish, and of the permanent undersecretary, Thomas Henry Burke, by Irish patriots (6 May). 'Kilmainham Treaty' between Gladstone and Parnell (May).

Egyptian Revolt. Battle of Kassassin (28 August): British defeated Egyptian attack; British fleet bombarded Alexandria; Britain occupied the Suez Canal Zone (until 1955); Battle of Tel-el-Kebir: Wolseley defeated Arabi Pasha.

Hague Convention established a three-mile limit for territorial waters.

Foundation of Selwyn College, Cambridge, in memory of the first bishop of New Zealand, George Selwyn.

Foundation of the London Polytechnic by Quintin Hogg.

Foundation of the Royal University of Ireland in Dublin (superseding the Queen's University in Ireland).

Foundation of the Society for Psychical Research.

Term 'telepathy' coined by Frederick Myers.

Foundation of the Church Army by Rev. Wilson Carlile.

Foundation of the *Dictionary of National Biography* by George Smith (first published 1885-1901).

The fourth Eddystone Lighthouse completed.

Gold found at Barberton, South Africa.

Institution of 'the Ashes' in cricket.

Deaths: Charles Darwin (19 April); the novelist Anthony Trollope (6 December).

1883

Foundation of the Primrose League, British Conservative organization by Lord Randolph Churchill.

Married Women's Property Act became law.

Sir Edward Sullivan became Lord Chancellor of Ireland (until 1885).

Sudan Campaign. Egyptian force under General Hicks massacred by Mahdists at Kashgal (3 November); British withdrew from Sudan.

Treaty of Ancon (20 October).

Foundation of the Fabian Society.

Inland parcel post began in Britain (1 August).

The Boys' Brigade founded in Glasgow by William Smith (4 October).

Publication of *Treasure Island* by Robert Louis Stevenson.

Artificial silk made by Sir Joseph Wilson Swan.

Discovery of gold-bearing lode in Transvaal.

The Eclipse Stakes horse race first run at Sandown Park.

Death in London of Karl Marx (14 March).

1884

Greenwich Mean Time made prime meridian of the world.

Third Reform Act (followed by redistribution next year).

British Somaliland made a British protectorate (until 1960).

Convention of London between Britain and the Transvaal: Boer independence strengthened.

Establishment of British protectorate over Papua, southern area of Papua New Guinea.

Berlin Conference of the Powers regarding Africa.

Sir Evelyn Baring (Lord Cromer) became consul-general in Egypt.

Sudan Campaign. Mahdist siege of General Gordon's garrison in Khartoum began; British defeated Mahdists at Battle of Tamai (13 March) and Battle of Trinkitat or El Teb (29 March).

Foundation of the National Society for the Prevention of Cruelty to Children (NSPCC) by Rev. Benjamin Waugh.

The term 'Industrial Revolution' for the period of 1760 to 1840 coined by Arnold Toynbee.

Completion of Revised Version of the Bible.

Artificial leather first manufactured in Britain.
Invention of a steam turbine to drive a high-speed electric generator by Charles Parsons.
Three-wheeled motorcycle built by Edward Butler.
Gold found at Witwatersrand, South Africa.

1885

Salisbury became prime minister (until 1886).
Bechuanaland became a British protectorate.
Indian National Congress founded.
Lord Roberts became commander-in-chief India (until 1893).
Riel's Second Rebellion in Canada under Louis Riel: rebels withstood attack at Battle of Fish Creek (24 April); Battle of Batoche (9–12 May): rebels defeated; Riel executed.
Sudan Campaign. Battle of Abu Klea (17 January): British troops withstood attack by a Mahdist force; Battle of Gubat or Abu Kru (19 January): British troops withstood Mahdist attack to reach the Nile; fall of Khartoum (26 January): General Gordon, governor of the Sudan (from 1877) killed; Battle of Kirbekan (10 February): British attacked and defeated Mahdist-held heights of Kirbekan; Battle of Hashin (20 March): British defeat of Mahdist army; Battle of Tofrek (22 March): Mahdist attack on British and Indian troops failed.
Foundation of Toynbee Hall in London in memory of Arnold Toynbee.
First performance of *The Mikado* by Gilbert and Sullivan.
Publication of *King Solomon's Mines* by H. Rider Haggard.
Manganese steel discovered by Robert Hadfield.
Rover 'safety' bicycle appeared.
Legalization of professional football (20 July).

1886

Gladstone became prime minister. He introduced his first Home Rule for Ireland Bill: defeated in Commons.
Salisbury again prime minister (until 1892).
Royal Niger Company formed.
The Plan of Campaign in Ireland.
Britain annexed Upper Burma.
Refoundation at Oxford University of Mansfield College (formerly Spring Hill College, Birmingham).

The game of bridge being played in England.

Cruft's dog show first held in London (10 March).

Publication of *Little Lord Fauntleroy* by Frances Hodgson Burnett.

Construction completed (began 1873) of the Severn tunnel.

Official opening of the Mersey railway tunnel by the Prince of Wales (20 January).

The *Gluckauf*, prototype of an oil tanker, built on Tyneside.

Gold rush in the Transvaal, South Africa.

The present Hockey Association formed.

1887

Jubilee of Queen Victoria.

The Labour Electoral Association (one of the forerunners of the Labour Party) formed by the TUC.

First Colonial Conference of the prime ministers of dominions.

The Maldives in the Indian Ocean came under British protection.

Opening of the second Tay Bridge, the longest railway bridge in Britain (20 June).

1888

Foundation of the Scottish Labour Party by Keir Hardie.

British protectorate declared over parts of Borneo, Brunei.

Christmas Island annexed by Britain.

Parnell Commission to investigate Parnell's authorship of a letter in *The Times* playing down the Phoenix Park murders. Vindication of Parnell.

The Gambia again made an independent British Crown Colony.

Signature of convention on Suez Canal.

A series of unsolved murders committed on women in London by 'Jack the Ripper'.

County Councils created in Britain.

Gregg's shorthand invented by John Gregg.

Foundation of *The Star* newspaper (absorbed by *The Evening News* 1960).

First detection of radio signals.

The pneumatic tyre perfected by John Boyd Dunlop.

Formation of the English Football League (22 March). Matches first played 8 September.

Formation of the Lawn Tennis Association.

1889

Ministry of Agriculture, Fisheries and Food (formerly Board of Agriculture) formed.

British South Africa Company formed.

Charles Stewart Parnell involved in the O'Shea divorce case.

Foundation of the Museums Association in London.

Foundation of the Women's Franchise League by Mrs Emmeline Pankhurst.

Influenza pandemic (until 1890).

Publication completed (began 1879) of Grove's *Dictionary of Music and Musicians*.

Publication of *Three Men in a Boat* by Jerome K. Jerome.

Lake Edward in Uganda discovered by Sir Henry Stanley.

Deaths: Wilkie Collins (23 September); Robert Browning (12 December).

1890

Formal declaration of Zanzibar as a British protectorate following the sultan placing it under British protection.

Britain ceded Heligoland to Germany.

Publication of *The Golden Bough* by Sir James Frazer.

The Daily Graphic newspaper founded (absorbed by *Daily Sketch* 1925).

First comic paper, *Comic Cuts*, published (17 May).

Forth Rail Bridge completed (begun 1883) by William Arrol, to designs by John Fowler and Benjamin Baker. Officially opened by the Prince of Wales (4 March).

Invention of the solid fuel injection principle by Herbert Ackroyd-Stuart.

Opening of the first electric underground public railway line (City and South London Railway) (18 December) between King William St and Stockwell.

Death of Cardinal Newman (11 August).

1891

Agreement between Britain and Portugal regarding East Africa. Nyasaland (now Malawi) constituted as the British Central Africa Protectorate. Establishment of constitutional government in Zanzibar. Foundation of the British colony of Southern Rhodesia by the British South Africa Company.

Baccarat case tried in June: Prince of Wales gave evidence concerning gambling at Tranby Croft.

Completion of New Scotland Yard by Norman Shaw.

Foundation of the Romanes Lectures at Oxford University by George Romanes.

First charity street collection made in Manchester for lifeboats (8 October).

The Baptist Union of Great Britain and Ireland formed.

The Kelmscott Press founded by William Morris (wound up1898).

Cordite, invented by Abel and Dewar, adopted by the Government.

Electrification of trams in England began in Leeds.

Synthetic rubber first produced by William Tilden.

Telephone service between London and Paris opened.

Foundation of the National Sporting Club.

Deaths: the pioneering travel agent Thomas Cook (18 July); Charles Stewart Parnell (6 October).

1892

Gladstone prime minister (until 1894) after a general election.

Keir Hardie elected Member of Parliament (until 1895).

Gilbert and Ellice Islands in the Western Pacific proclaimed a British protectorate (annexed by Britain 1915 and remained a colony until 1975; achieved full independence as Kiribati 1979).

Grenfell Mission founded in Labrador by Wilfred Grenfell.

Indian Councils Act.

Bibliographical Society founded in London.

Foundation of Reading University (as the University Extension College).

Foundation of *The Westminster Gazette* newspaper (absorbed by *The Daily News* 1928).

Linotype first made in England.

'Gentleman Jim' Corbett became the first world heavyweight boxing champion under Queensberry Rules (7 September).

Death of Lord Tennyson (6 October).

1893

Marriage of the Duke of York (later George V) and Princess Mary of Teck (6 July).

The Independent Labour Party founded by Keir Hardie.

Durand Line defining the frontier between India and Afghanistan
  determined.
Establishment of the Solomon Islands as a British protectorate (until
  1899).
Gladstone's second Home Rule for Ireland Bill rejected by the Lords.
Matabele War in Rhodesia.
Natal granted responsible government.
The Gaelic League founded in Dublin.
Bering Sea arbitration between Britain and the United States.
Foundation of St Hilda's College, Oxford.
First performance of *The Second Mrs Tanqueray* by Sir Arthur Pinero.
World's first elevated railway opened at Liverpool (4 February).

1894

Birth of a son (later Edward VIII) to Prince George (later George V)
  and Princess Mary.
Gladstone resigned: Rosebery became prime minister. Harcourt's
  budget introduced death duties (2 August).
Use permitted of postcards with adhesive stamps.
British protectorate over Uganda (until 1896).
Motor vehicles became common.
First publication of *The Yellow Book* quarterly (until 1897).
Publication of *The Prisoner of Zenda* by Anthony Hope.
Official opening by Queen Victoria of the Manchester Ship Canal (21
  May, construction began 1887).
Opening of Tower Bridge in London (30 June).
The inert gas argon discovered by Lord Lister and Sir William Ramsay.
Opening of the first Penny Bazaar (Marks and Spencer's) in Man-
  chester (28 September).
Death of Robert Louis Stevenson in Samoa (3 December).

1895

Birth of a second son (later Duke of York and George VI) to Prince
  George (later George V) and Princess Mary.
Salisbury again prime minister (until 1902): Conservative victory at
  general election.
Chitral Campaign in India. British force defeated Indians at Malakand
  Pass (3 April).
Federation of Malaya formed.

Jameson Raid, Transvaal, led by Dr Leander Starr Jameson (29
  December to 2 January 1896): Cecil Rhodes forced to resign as
  prime minister of South Africa.
  British ultimatum to the Transvaal.
Third Ashanti War began (ended 1900).
Booksellers Association of Great Britain and Ireland founded as the
  Associated Booksellers (assumed present name 1948).
Foundation of the National Trust for places of historic interest or
  natural beauty.
First performance of *The Importance of Being Earnest* by Oscar Wilde.
Foundation of the London Promenade Concerts by Sir Henry Wood
  (6 October).
Helium obtained by William Ramsay..
Wireless telegraphy brought about by Marconi.
Secession of Rugby League from Rugby Union (as Northern Union;
  name changed 1922).
Death in London of Friedrich Engels (5 August).

1896

Outbreak of plague in India.
Sudan Campaign. Battle of Ferkeh (7 June): Egyptian and British
  troops under Kitchener defeated Mahdists.
Franco-British treaty regarding Siam.
Foundation by Queen Victoria of the Royal Victorian Order.
Alfred Austin became poet laureate.
Publication of A *Shropshire Lad* by A. E. Housman.
The Daily Mail newspaper founded by Lord Northcliffe (4 May).
Alpha and beta rays discovered by Lord Rutherford.
Marconi patented wireless telegraphy (2 June).
Gold found in Rabbit Creek in the Klondike, Canada (17 August);
  beginning of gold rush.

1897

Queen Victoria's Diamond Jubilee.
Northwest Frontier Campaign. Revolt of tribes on Indian northwest
  frontier; Battle of Dargai (20 October): Heights of Dargai stormed
  by British. Indian frontier rebellion ended.
Sudan Campaign. Battle of Abu Hamed (7 August): Mahdist troops
  defeated by Egyptian troops under British officers.

Zululand annexed to Natal (30 December).

Constitution of Sheffield University as a university college.

Foundation of the Royal Automobile Club as the Automobile Club of
   Great Britain (10 August)..

Official opening of the Tate Gallery (21 July).

Publication of *Dracula* by Bram Stoker.

Electron discovered by Joseph John Thomson.

Invention of the first turbine-propelled ship by Charles Parsons.

The national standard metre established in Britain.

1898

Irish Local Government Act.

Lord Minto made governor-general of Canada (until 1904).

Sudan Campaign. Battle of Atbara (8 April): British and Egyptian
   army under Sir Herbert Kitchener defeated Mahdists; Fashoda
   Incident when French occupied British fort (10 July); Battle of
   Omdurman (2 September): Kitchener's army defeated Dervishes;
   Sudan reconquered.

Britain obtained 99-year lease of Hong Kong from China (9 June).

Idea of garden cities introduced into England by Sir Ebenezer Howard.

Official opening of the Tate Gallery (21 July), founded by Sir Henry
   Tate.

Definition by Oliver Lodge of the basic principles of selective radio
   tuning.

Discovery of the element xenon and the inert gas krypton by William
   Ramsay and Morris Travers; the gaseous element neon discovered
   by Ramsay.

Deaths: Lewis Carroll (14 January); William Gladstone (19 May).

1899

United Irish League formed.

Lord Curzon became viceroy of India (until 1905).

The Gulf state of Kuwait became a British protectorate.

John Rylands Library founded in Manchester by the widow of John
   Rylands.

Revival of morris dancing led by Cecil Sharp who saw a demonstration of it at Headington, Oxford (26 December).

Second Boer War (11 October, ended 31 May 1902).

   October: beginning of sieges of the British by the Boers at

Mafeking (12) and Kimberley (15); British garrison at Mafeking commanded by Baden-Powell; Battle of Talana Hill or Battle of Dundee, north Natal (20), Boers defeated; Battle of Elandslaagte (21): Boers defeated; British troops prevent Boer attack on forces retreating from Talana Hill (24); Battle of Farquhar's Farm at Ladysmith (29): British defeated by Boers.

November: Siege of British at Ladysmith began (2); Battle of Graspan or Enslin (25): successful British attack on Boer position; Battle of Modder River (28): Boers defeated by Lord Methuen.

December: Battle of Stormberg (10): British defeated by Boers; Battle of Magersfontein: Boers defeated Methuen (11); Battle of Colenso (15): British attack on Boers failed.

Foundation of the National Physical Laboratory.

1900

Second Boer War. *January*: Boers attacked Ladysmith (6); Field Marshal Lord Roberts took command of British forces (10); Battle of Spion Kop (19–24): Boers defeated General Buller in his second attempt to relieve the siege of Ladysmith.

February: Battle of Vaalkranz (5–7): Buller's third attempt to break Boer lines failed; Kimberley relieved (15); Battle of Paardeberg (18–27): Boers under Cronje defeated by British under Kitchener and surrendered to Lord Roberts; Relief of Ladysmith (28).

March: Battle of Driefontein (10): British under Roberts defeated Boers; Boers defeated by British at Karee (29); British troops ambushed by Boers at Sanna's Post (31).

April: British defeated at Battle of Reddersberg (3); British besieged by Boers at Wepener (9); relieved (25).

May: Relief of Mafeking (17); Annexation of Orange Free State (26); Boer victory at Battle of Lindley (27); unsuccessful British attack on Boers at Senekal (29).

June: Battle of Diamond Hill (11–12): British attack under Roberts on Boers successful.

August: Battle of Elands River (4–15): Boer attack on Australians relieved by Kitchener; Battle of Dalmanutha (21–28): British defeated Boers and entered Machadodorp.

October: Annexation of Transvaal (25).

The Labour Party founded (as the Labour Representation Committee)

in London (27-28 February): present name adopted 1906. Ramsay
  MacDonald named as its secretary.
Unionist victory at general election ('Khaki Election', 28 September-
  16 October).
Tonga in the South Pacific became a British protectorate.
  Royal Niger Company's territories taken over by the Crown. British
  protectorate over Lagos and Nigeria.
Boxer Rising: Chinese attack on foreign legations in Peking (13 June
  and July). Peking taken by international force.
Charter granted to Birmingham University.
United Free Church of Scotland founded by union of Free and United
  Presbyterian Churches.
Excavations started at Knossos on Crete by Sir John Evans, leading to
  his discovery of the Minoan Civilization.
First performance of *The Dream of Gerontius* by Sir Edward Elgar.
Opening of the Wallace Collection in London.
Publication of *The Daily Express* began.
Central London electric railway opened (27 June).
Development of the thermionic valve by John Fleming.
Davis Cup for tennis first competed for (8 August): won by the USA.
Deaths: the art critic John Ruskin (20 January); the composer Sir
  Arthur Sullivan (22 November); the playwright Oscar Wilde in
  Paris (30 November).

1901

Death of Queen Victoria (22 January): Prince of Wales became king
  as Edward VII. His son George became Prince of Wales (later
  George V).
Second Boer War. *June*: denunciation of use of concentration camps
  as prison camps for Afrikaner women and children by Campbell-
  Bannerman (14).
  October: Boers invade Cape Colony.
Commonwealth of Australia founded (1 January).
Britain annexed Ashanti, former West African kingdom, and incorpo-
  rated it within the colony of the Gold Coast (25 September).
Northwest Frontier Province of North Pakistan made part of British
  India (until 1947).
Taff Vale decision of Lords affecting legal position of trade unions.

British Standards Institution founded as the Engineering Standards Committee (incorporated by Royal Charter 1929).

Launch of the first Royal Navy submarine (2 October).

Radio signals first sent across the Atlantic by Marconi (from Cornwall to Newfoundland, 12 December).

Boxing legalized in England.

1902

Foundation of the Order of Merit by Edward VII (23 June).

Resignation of Salisbury: Balfour became prime minister (until 1905).

Empire Day (later Commonwealth Day) first celebrated on Queen Victoria's birthday (24 May).

Second Boer War. Signature of the Treaty of Vereeniging between Britain and the Boers ended the war (31 May).

Foundation of Southampton University (gained university status 1952).

British Academy granted charter (8 August).

Cancer Research Institute founded.

Education Act for England and Wales: keen opposition by Nonconformists.

King Edward VII Land, Antarctica, identified by Robert Scott.

Coronation Cup horse race first run at Epsom.

Death of Cecil Rhodes (26 March). Rhodes Scholarships at Oxford University provided for by his will.

1903

Chamberlain resigned as Secretary for the Colonies in order to advocate Protection.

Irish Land Purchase Act.

Demolition of Newgate Prison completed (began 1902).

First session of Manchester University formally opened (6 October).

Foundation of the militant Women's Social and Political Union by Mrs Emmeline Pankhurst and Christabel Pankhurst to agitate for votes for women.

Letchworth, first garden city in England, founded.

The evidence of fingerprints first used in securing a criminal conviction (13 September).

Opening of Westminster Cathedral (consecrated 1910).

Randall Davidson became archbishop of Canterbury (until 1928).

First performance of *Man and Superman* by Bernard Shaw.

Publication of *The Riddle of the Sands* by Erskine Childers.

Publication of *The Daily Mirror* began (2 November).

British car registration introduced.

Sugar Convention abolished sugar bounties.

Commander Robert Falcon Scott and Lieutenant Ernest Shackleton travel farther towards the South Pole than any previous expedition.

Deaths: Herbert Spencer; the American-born painter James McNeill Whistler (17 July).

*c.*1903

Internal secretion of hormones discovered by William Bayliss and Ernest Starling.

1904

Anglo-French Entente signed, aimed at solving all outstanding grievances.

Somali Expedition. Battle of Jidballi (10 January): British attacked and defeated Somali forces.

British military expedition to Tibet captures Lhasa (3 August). Anglo-Tibetan Treaty signed giving Britain exclusive trading rights (7 September).

Dogger Bank incident between Britain and Russia: settled peaceably.

Triple Entente between England, France and Russia established (until 1917).

Booklets of stamps first issued in Britain (16 March).

Licensing Act for England and Wales.

Abbey Theatre, Dublin, founded (burned down 1952, rebuilt 1966).

First concert of the London Symphony Orchestra (9 June).

First performance of *Peter Pan* by James Barrie.

Diode valve invented by Sir John Fleming.

Electrification of the Metropolitan Railway in London between Baker Street and Harrow.

Northern Underground Line in London opened (as the Great Northern and City Railway).

Death of the explorer Stanley.

1905

Legal recognition of office of prime minister.

Liberal leader, Campbell-Bannerman, became prime minister.

Sinn Fein formed by Arthur Griffith (28 November).
District of Alberta and Saskatchewan became Provinces of Canada.
Lord Minto made viceroy of India (until 1910).
Dartmouth College (Britannia Royal Naval College) opened.
Automobile Association founded (26 June).
Sheffield University gained university status.
Aldwych Theatre opened.
Publication of *Kipps* by H. G. Wells.
Dreadnought warships introduced by Lord Fisher.
Inauguration of a river steamboat service on the Thames.
Death of the social reformer Dr Thomas Barnardo (19 September).

1906

General election in Britain: overwhelming Liberal victory. First
  Labour Members of Parliament.
Self-government granted to Transvaal.
Beginning of construction of Rosyth naval base in Scotland.
Trades Disputes Act reversed Taff Vale decision.
Women's suffrage movement in Britain gathers strength.
John Bull magazine founded by Horatio Bottomley (12 May).
Opening of the Bakerloo Line of the London Underground (10
  March) and the Piccadilly Line (15 December).
Official opening of the Vauxhall Bridge in London (26 May).
Discovery of vitamins by Frederick Hopkins.

1907

Cullinan diamond (found in 1905) presented to Edward VII on behalf
  of the people of Transvaal (9 November).
Mahatma Ghandi led civil disobedience movement in South Africa.
New Zealand declared a Dominion within the British Empire (26
  September).
Self-government granted to Orange River Colony as the Orange Free
  State.
Second Hague Peace Conference.
Territorial and Reserve Forces Act. Inauguration of the Territorial
  Army at Buckingham Palace (26 October).
Boy Scout movement, devised by Lord Baden-Powell, began with
  first camp in Dorset (August).
Small Holdings and Allotments Act for England and Wales.

Foundation of *The Nation* periodical (absorbed into the *New States-man* 1931).

First official recognition of taxi cabs.

The Cunard ship *Mauretania,* the world's largest liner, sailed on her maiden voyage.

First TT motorycycle race held on the Isle of Man (28 May).

Brooklands motor racecourse opened (6 July, closed 1939).

Deaths: William Howard Russell; the scientist Lord Kelvin (17 December).

1908

King Edward VII visited Russia: the first monarch to do so.

Resignation of Campbell-Bannerman because of ill health; Asquith became prime minister (8 April, until 7 December 1916). Death of Campbell-Bannerman (22 April).

Mass demonstration of suffragettes in Hyde Park, London.

Beginning of the London Naval Conference on war at sea (ended 1909).

Launch of the first British diesel submarine (16 May).

First woman mayor in England: Elizabeth Garrett Anderson elected mayor of Aldeburgh (9 November).

Foundation of the National Farmers' Union (10 December).

Franco-British Exhibition in London.

Old Age Pensions introduced in Britain.

British Red Cross Society received Royal Charter.

Boy Scouts founded by Lord Baden-Powell.

Opening of the Public Trustee Office in London.

Publication of *The Wind in the Willows* by Kenneth Grahame.

Geiger counter invented by Hans Geiger and Lord Rutherford.

Opening of the Rotherhithe to Stepney tunnel under the Thames (12 June).

Opening of the fourth official modern Olympic Games in London (13 July).

The first unofficial Olympic Winter Games held in London.

1909

Radical budget ('People's Budget') introduced by Lloyd George as Chancellor of the Exchequer (April): rejected by the Lords (November). Introduction of a Bill to curb the power of the House of Lords. Trade Boards Act to deal with sweated labour. Osborne Judgment preventing use of trade union funds for political action.

The Old Age Pensions Act came into force (1 January).

Signature of Declaration of London, concerning maritime law.

Port of London Authority established.

First Rally and Conference of the Boy Scout movement (4 September).

King's Police Medal instituted by Royal Warrant.

Queen's College, Belfast, became Queen's University, Belfast.

Foundation of the National University of Ireland in Dublin (31 October), previously the Royal University of Ireland.

The Daily Sketch founded by Edward Hulton.

First crossing of the English Channel by aeroplane (27 July) by Blériot: rapid development of aviation.

Trolleybus first used.

Anglo-Persian Oil Company (now British Petroleum) formed.

Foundation of Selfridge's department store in Oxford Street, London, by Gordon Selfridge (15 March).

South magnetic pole reached by the Shackleton Expedition (16 January).

Lonsdale Boxing Belt founded by Lord Lonsdale.

Death of the writer George Meredith (18 May).

1910

Constitutional Conference between Government and Opposition regarding Lords' veto: failed.

Death of Edward VII from bronchitis (6 May): his son became king of Britain as George V.

General election (January): Liberal victory: the Liberals clung on to power as the crisis over the People's Budget and the power of the House of Lords escalated. Lloyd George's budget passed.

The creation of the Union of South Africa (31 May); creation of the Orange Free State and Transvaal as Provinces of South Africa; merger of Natal in the Union of South Africa.

Airmail post first organized in Britain.

Girl Guides Association funded by Sir Robert Baden-Powell.

Labour Exchanges established in Britain.

Dr Crippen hanged for the murder of his wife in London (23 November).

Appearance of Halley's Comet (named after Edmund Halley): first time it was photographed.

Isotopes first identified by Joseph John Thomson.

Foundation of Textile Institute in Manchester.

Captain Robert Falcon Scott set out on expedition to the South Pole (15 June).

Deaths: Florence Nightingale (13 August); the painter William Holman Hunt.

1911

Andrew Bonar Law chosen to succeed Balfour as leader of the Conservative Party.

Coronation of George V (23 June).

Parliament Act passed after King George V had agreed to creation of peers on advice of prime minister: absolute veto of Lords ended. National Insurance Act passed (14 December). Payment of Members of Parliament introduced in Britain.

Ramsay MacDonald elected chairman of the Labour Party to succeed Keir Hardie.

Zambia unified as Northern Rhodesia.

Great labour unrest, culminating in a national railway strike.

Sidney Street Siege: armed troops and police besiege an Anarchist hideout in a house in Sidney Street, London.

Copyright Act establishes protection of an author's work for fifty years after death.

English Folk Dance Society founded by Cecil Sharp (succeeded 1932 by English Folk Dance and Song Society).

Development of the self-starter mechanism for cars by Charles Kettering.

First escalator in England installed at Earls Court Station.

Invention of the Wilson Cloud Chamber by Charles Wilson.

Amundsen reached the South Pole (14 December) ahead of Scott.

Death of Sir William Gilbert (29 May).

1912

Ireland. Mass rallies in Ulster to protest at proposals for Home Rule for Ireland (January); Third Home Rule for Ireland Bill passed by the Commons (May); 'Solemn Covenant' to oppose Home Rule signed at a mass rally of Ulster loyalists led by Sir Edward Carson (September).

Welsh Disestablishment Bill introduced: passed through Commons but rejected by Lords.

Establishment of the Royal Flying Corps (14 May).

Establishment of Queen Alexandra's Day (26 June).

Frederick Seddon hanged for murder.

Militant suffragettes riot in the West End of London.

National strike of coal-miners in Britain: settled by passage of Coal Mines (Minimum Wage) Act which established the principle of a minimum wage.

The *Titanic* sank in the Atlantic on her maiden voyage (15 April): a loss of 1,513 lives.

Beginning of National Insurance in Britain (15 July).

The Daily Herald newspaper first published (16 April).

First Royal Command performance held in London (1 July).

Announcement of the 'discovery' of Piltdown man (18 December, proved a hoax 1953/55).

Development of the theory of isotopes by Frederick Soddy.

First crossing of the English Channel of an aeroplane piloted by a woman, the American Harriet Quimby.

Identification of the proton unit of positive charge, the hydrogen nucleus of the atom, by Rutherford.

Discovery in Antarctica of King George V Land by Douglas Mawson and of Queen Mary Land by Captain Davis.

Robert Scott reached the South Pole (18 January) but discovered that Amundsen had reached it on 14 December 1911. Scott and his companions died on the return journey.

Death of General Booth, founder of the Salvation Army (20 August); he was succeeded as General by his son, William Bramwell Booth.

Deaths: Lord Lister, pioneer of antisepsis (10 February); the composer Samuel Coleridge-Taylor.

1913

Last renewal of Triple Alliance.

Second Irish Volunteers formed.

Introduction of sickness, unemployment and maternity benefit (15 January).

Death of the suffragette Emily Davison after she threw herself in front of the king's horse during the Derby (4 June).

Emily Duncan appointed first British woman stipendiary magistrate (16 May).

Trades Union Act empowered trade unions to raise political fund, safe-guarding rights of minorities.

Opening of the first Chelsea Flower Show in London (20 May).

Foundation of the *New Statesman* periodical.

Death of the poet laureate Alfred Austin. Robert Bridges became poet laureate.

1914

Buckingham Palace conference on the future of Ireland called by George V.

Irish Home Rule Act created a separate parliament in Ireland with some MPs in Westminster. Home Rule Bill and Welsh Disestablishment Bill passed, but operation suspended till end of World War I.

Mutiny of the Curragh, Ireland (March).

The Simla Conference of British, Chinese and Tibetan representatives delineated the northeast frontier of India, named after the British representative, Sir Henry McMahon.

Foundation of Rotary International in Britain.

Cub Scout movement began (2 February).

Formation of the Royal Naval Air Service (23 June).

First flag day held in England (3 October).

World War I (28 July–11 November 1918). *June*: Murder of Archduke Francis Ferdinand, heir to Austrian throne, in Serajevo, capital of Bosnia (28).

July: Austria declared war against Serbia (28).

August: Germany declared war against Russia (1); Germany declared war against France (3); German invasion of Belgium (4); Britain declared war against Germany in support of France and Belgium (4); British Expeditionary Force landed in France under Sir John French and suffered heavy casualties at the Battle of Mons (20-31); Japan declared war on Germany (23); Battle of Heligoland between British and German fleets (27–28).

September: Germans capture Rheims (5); Battle of the Marne (5-9); trench warfare began on Aisne salient (13); three British cruisers sunk by a U-boat (22).

October: First Battle of Ypres (12-11 November).

November: Battle of Coronel: British squadron defeated by

Germans (1); Britain declared war against Turkey and annexed Cyprus (5); Death of Lord Roberts in France (14).

December: Royal Navy destroyed German squadron in the Battle of the Falkland Islands (8); British protectorate over Egypt (17) and Kuwait proclaimed (17).

Lord Kitchener became British Secretary for War.

Germany surrendered Togoland to Britain and French; German areas of Papua New Guinea came under Australian control.

1915

World War I. *January*: institution of the Military Cross (l); German Zeppelin raid on Norfolk towns (19); British sank German battleship *Blucher* in North Sea (24).

February: German submarine blockade of Britain began (2); Imperial troops repulsed Turkish attack on Suez Canal (2).

March: Britain declared blockade of German ports (l); Battle of Neuve Chapelle (10-13); naval attack on Dardanelles aborted (22).

April: Second Battle of Ypres (22-25 May); Germans used gas for the first time on the Western Front (22); British, ANZAC and French troops landed at Gallipoli (25).

May: sinking of the Cunard liner *Lusitania* (7); Battle of Aubers Ridge (9-25); Italy declared war on Austria (22); British coalition government formed under Asquith (26); first air raid on London (31).

June: British pilot Reginald Warneford awarded Victoria Cross for destroying a Zeppelin.

July: Germans advanced farther into Poland (3); General Botha accepted surrender of all German forces in South-west Africa (9).

August: Allied forces met stubborn resistance at Gallipoli (13); Italy declared war against Turkey (20); Brest-Litovsk fell to the Germans (30).

September: Allies breeched German lines at Champagne and at Loos in Flanders (26); Turks defeated at Kut-el-Amara in Mesopotamia (28).

October: Russia began campaign against Bulgaria (8); British nurse Edith Cavell executed by Germans as a spy (12).

November: Italians suffered heavy losses at Isonzo River (10); Serbia occupied by German-Austrian and Bulgarian forces (28).

December: Sir Douglas Haig replaced Sir John French as British
  commander on the Western Front (15); French and British troops
  occupied Salonika (13); Allied troops began evacuation of Gallipoli
  (20).
Foundation of St Dunstan's Home for blinded soldiers and sailors by
  Sir Arthur Pearson.
Requirement for photographs in passports introduced (1 February).
Women's Institute organization founded in Britain (11 September).
Deaths: the poet Rupert Brooke from blood poisoning (23 April);
  Keir Hardie, the founder of the Labour Party (26 September); the
  cricketer W. G. Grace who had scored a hundred centuries between
  1864 and 1895 (23 October).

1916

World War I. *January*: conscription introduced in Britain (6);
  withdrawal of troops from Gallipoli completed (8); tanks first tested
  and named (29).
February: Allies completed occupation of Germany colony of
  Cameroons (18); Battle of Verdun between Germans and French
  began (21).
April: British forces surrendered to Turks after fall of Kut-el-Amara
  (29).
May: Battle of Jutland between the British and German fleets, only
  major sea battle of the war, in which both sides claimed victory
  (31); official adoption of daylight saving (pioneered by William
  Willett) as British Summer Time to conserve coal stocks (21).
June: Lord Kitchener drowned when cruiser *Hampshire* was struck
  by a mine off Orkney (6).
September: tanks first used by the British Army on the Western
  Front (15); Allies launched new offensive in the Balkans (18);
  destruction of Zeppelin L21 at Cuffley (3) and Zeppelin L33 in
  Essex (24).
October: Allies occupied Athens (16); Captain T. E. Lawrence
  arrived in Jeddah to offer British support for Arab revolt against
  Turkey (16); Second Battle of Verdun began (24).
November: Battle of the Somme (1-18).
December: Asquith resigned and Lloyd George formed war cabinet
  as new prime minister (7); end of the Battle of Verdun (16).

Ireland. Easter Rising in Ireland, led by Padraic Pearse (23–29 April).
  Arrest of Roger Casement (24 April), executed for treason (3
  August). Padraic Pearse court-martialled and shot.
The Persian Gulf State of Qatar became a British protectorate (until
  1971).
ANZAC Day first celebrated in London (25 April).
Foundation of the National Savings Movement (19 February).
Closure of Sadler's Wells Theatre, London.
Discovery of Proxima Centauri, the star nearest Earth, by Robert
  Innes.
Invention of stainless steel by Harry Brearley.
Death of Sir Joseph Beecham, manufacturer of pharmaceuticals.
Deaths: the American-born British writer Henry James (28 February);
  the composer George Butterworth.

1917

World War I. *February*: unrestricted submarine warfare begins (1).
  March: British troops occupied Baghdad (11); British defeated
  Turks near Gaza (27); Women's Army Auxiliary Corps founded
  (28).
  April: United States declared war on Germany (6); Battle of Arras
  (9–14); Vimy Ridge captured by Canadian troops (10).
  June: Messines Ridge taken by British (7); German aircraft carried
  out first bombing raid on London (14); first American troops land in
  France (26); General Edmund Allenby assumed Palestine command
  (29).
  July: authorization given for the formation of the British Army's
  Tank Corps (28); third Battle of Ypres began (31).
  Mustard gas first used by the Germans (July).
  October: Passchendaele captured by British (6); Hindenburg lines
  smashed on 10-mile front (20).
  December: Jerusalem taken by the British (9); Russo-German
  armistice (15).
Adoption of the name Windsor instead of Saxe-Coburg-Gotha by the
  British royal family (17 July).
Order of the British Empire founded by George V.
  First DBE (Dame of the British Empire) created: Marchioness of
  Londonderry, founder and director of the Women's Legion.

Balfour Declaration, in favour of the creation of a Jewish national home in Palestine, made by the British government (2 November).

Constitution of Newfoundland as a Dominion (created a Province 1949).

Foundation of the Whitley Councils regarding British labour conditions mainly by John Whitley, Speaker of the House of Commons.

First investigation of the aeronautic spin by Frederick Lindemann.

1918

World War I. *January*: President Wilson outlined to Congress American war aims in his Fourteen Points (8/9).

March: German offensive against British on the Somme opened (21); Battle of Arras (21–4 April).

April: establishment of the Royal Air Force from the Royal Flying Corps and Royal Naval Air Service (1); second German offensive against British (9–25); British naval raid on Belgian ports of Zeebrugge and Ostend (23/22); the League of Nations founded (28).

May: Battle of the Aisne began (27): Germans attacked British and French.

June: German advance on the Aisne halted (6).

August: Allied offensive near Amiens resulted in German collapse (8).

September: Turkish army destroyed at Megiddo (19); Battle of Passchendaele in Belgium (28); Bulgarian signed armistice (29); Allied breakthrough along the whole Western Front (30); Congress of Aix-la-Chapelle opened (30).

October: T. E. Lawrence led Arabs into Damascus (1); conquest of Palestine from the Turks completed; Germans accepted the Fourteen Points (23); Italian advance (24); surrender of Turkey (30).

November: Austria accepted peace terms (4); Kaiser abdicated and escaped to Holland (9); armistice signed by Germany (11); German fleet surrendered at sea (14); Congress of Aix-la-Chapelle closed (21).

December: Rhineland occupied by Allied troops (6–9).

Ireland. Irish Parliament formed in Dublin. Sir John French made lord lieutenant of Ireland (until 1921).

The Labour Party adopted its constitution.

Influenza pandemic (until 1919).

Leicester University founded (as the Leicester, Leicestershire and
  Rutland College); renamed University College, Leicester in 1927;
  gained university status 1957.

Women over thirty allowed to vote for the first time, conditional on
  educational and property qualifications, at the general election
  ('coupon election') (14 December): Liberal win; Lloyd George
  became prime minister of a Liberal government.

Election of the first woman to the House of Commons when Countess
  Markievicz was elected as Sinn Fein member for a Dublin constitu-
  ency: she refused to take the oath of alliegiance to the king and
  therefore could not taker her seat.

National Savings stamps first issued for sale (8 July).

Publication of *Eminent Victorians* by Lytton Strachey.

Death in World War I of the poet Wilfred Owen.

1919

World War I aftermath. Peace Conference in Paris (18 January);
  interned German fleet of battleships scuttled at Scapa Flow (21
  June); Germany signed Treaty of Versailles (28 June); the signato-
  ries of the Treaty of Versailles subscribed to the League of Nations
  (28 June); signature of the Treaty of Neuilly between the Allies and
  Bulgaria (27 November).

Dail Eireann, Irish Free State Chamber of Deputies, formed in Dublin
  (January); Irish Republican Army formed: Irish Volunteers merged
  with IRA.

Lloyd George announced plan for the partition of Ireland.

Nancy Astor became first woman MP to take her seat in the House of
  Commons (1 December).

Amritsar massacre of protesting Indians, 380 dead and over 1200
  wounded by British troops under General Dyer (13 April).

British mandate in Iraq (until 1921).

Former West African German colony of Cameroon divided into
  British Cameroons and French Cameroun (united as a republic
  1961).

Outbreak of Third Afghan War (3 May): signature of the Treaty of
  Rawalpindi (8 August) ended the war.

Formation of the Rover Scouts movement.

The term 'dole' applied to unemployment payments by *The Daily Mail*.

Disestablishment of the Church of Wales.

First publication of the periodical *John O'London's Weekly* (until 1954; revived 1959).

A daily air service between London and Paris inaugurated (25 August).

Atom split by Lord Rutherford; he was also the first to observe nuclear disintegration of nitrogen atoms.

Invention of the spectrograph by Francis Aston.

John Alcock and Arthur Brown flew non-stop across the Atlantic, arrived in County Galway 15 June.

First airship crossing of the Atlantic: R34 landed in New York State 6 July.

Deaths: Andrew Carnegie, Scottish-born American philanthropist (11 August); Sir John Alcock following a plane accident (18 December).

1920

Conscription ended in Britain (30 April).

Ireland. Government of Ireland Act: unacceptable to the south; administration of Northern Ireland by separate parliament and executive government established in the Act. 'Black and Tans' auxiliary police used for the first time against Irish republicans (2 January, ceased 1921). 'Bloody Sunday': IRA killed fourteen British soldiers in Ireland. Death in prison of the Irish patriot Terence MacSwiney following a hunger strike (1 November).

Kenya annexed to the British Crown as a colony (8 July).

League of Nations came into effect (1 January): Germany, Austria, Russia and Turkey excluded; American Senate voted against US membership. Signature of the Treaty of Trianon between Hungary and the Allies (4 June); Treaty of Sèvres concluded peace with Turkey and dissolved the Ottoman Empire (10 August).

Opening of the Royal Air Force College (5 February).

Admission of women to degrees at Oxford University.

Building of Welwyn Garden City.

First World Jamboree of Boy Scouts held in London.

Foundation of the Communist Party of Great Britain.

Foundation of the Royal Institute of International Affairs.

Horatio Bottomley imprisoned for fraud (until 1927).

Enthronement of the first archbishop of Wales (1 June)

First publication of *Time and Tide*, founded and edited by Lady Rhondda.

First significant example of a documentary film appeared: *Nanook of the North* by Robert Flaherty.

Montagu Norman became governor of the Bank of England.

Cenotaph, memorial to the death of both World Wars in Whitehall, London, unveiled (11 November).

1921

Ireland. Anglo-Irish Treaty setting up the Irish Free State, signed (6 December); Irish Free State established; division of the former kingdom of Ulster into Northern Ireland (Antrim, Armagh, Down, Fermanagh, Londonderry and Tyrone) and the republic of Ireland (Cavan, Donegal and Monaghan).

Limitation of Armaments Conference began in Washington (12 November, ended 6 February 1922).

Opening of the first Indian parliament (3 January); Lord Reading became viceroy of India (until 1926).

Anglo-Afghan Treaty concluded in Kabul by the Dobbs Mission (22 November).

British troops sent to quell rioting in Egypt.

British Legion (made Royal British Legion in 1971) founded by Earl Haig (14 May): it organized Poppy Day, first held 11 November.

First English birth control clinic opened in London.

First English woman barrister qualified (25 May).

Foundation of PEN International, world association of writers, in London.

Foundation of the British Broadcasting Company.

Insulin isolated by Frederick Banting and Charles Best.

King George V Dock, London, opened.

Death of John Boyd Dunlop, inventor of the pneumatic tyre (23 October).

1922

Ireland. Execution of Erskine Childers, Irish patriot; Michael Collins killed by Republicans (22 August).

Lloyd George resigned. Andrew Bonar Law became prime minister of a Conservative government after a general election (17 November).

League of Nations divided Togoland into British Togoland and
   French Togoland.
Abolition of the British protectorate over Egypt (6 February);
   recognition of independence (15 March).
Palestine proclaimed a British mandate (until 1948).
First skywriting in England carried out over Epsom Downs.
Establishment of 2LO broadcasting station in London (11 May).
   Regular broadcasts began 14 November. Daily news broadcasts
   began 23 December.
Introduction of the radio licence (1 November).
Completion of *The Forstye Saga* (began 1906) by John Galsworthy.
Discovery of the tomb of the ancient Egyptian pharoah Tutankhamun
   by Howard Carter (26 November).
Publication of *Just William* by Richmal Crompton and *The Waste
   Land* by T. S. Eliot.
Deaths: Sir Ernest Shackleton, Antarctic explorer, in South Georgia
   (5 January); Alfred Harmsworth, Lord Northcliffe, newspaper
   proprietor (14 August).

1923

Bonar Law resigned because of illness; Stanley Baldwin succeeded as
   prime minister (22 May).
General election (6 December): Conservatives won but as a minority
   government. Labour had the second highest number of seats.
Establishment of the first British local Record Office at Bedford.
Marriage of Lady Elizabeth Bowes-Lyon and the Duke of York, later
   George VI (26 April).
Big Ben chimes broadcast for the first time (31 December).
First publication of *Radio Times* (28 September).
Sir Arthur Bliss made Master of the King's Musick.
First English FA Cup final played at Wembley (28 April).

1924

Baldwin's Conservative government resigned. King George V asked
   Ramsay MacDonald to form the first Labour government (23
   January); the new government recognized the USSR (1 February).
Publication of the Zinoviev Letter purporting to be from Grigori
   Zinoviev, Russian leader of the Communist International, with plans
   for a Communist uprising in Britain (25 November).

General election (29 October): overwhelming Conservative victory; Baldwin became prime minister for the second time (until 1929).

Assam (incorporated into Bengal by 1914) became separate province.

Zambia made a British protectorate.

Dawes Plan for restructuring the payment of German reparations to the Allies agreed at the London Conference.

ASLIB (the Association of Special Libraries and Information Bureaux) founded.

British Empire Exhibition (Wembley Exhibition) held at Wembley, London (23 April–1 November).

Consecration of Liverpool Cathedral (19 July): building began 1904.

First appearance of a crossword in a British newspaper, *The Sunday Express*.

First transmission of radio photographs from Britain to the US.

Plans for a tunnel under the English Channel abandoned by the British government.

Cheltenham Gold Cup horse race first run.

Deaths: Frances Hodgson Burnett and E. E. Nesbit, children's authors; the Polish-born British writer Joseph Conrad (3 August).

1925

Dominions Office founded (assumed name of Commonwealth Relations Office in 1947).

Cyprus became a British Crown Colony.

Signature in London of the Treaty of Locarno, guaranteeing peace and frontiers in Europe (16 October).

British Summer Time made a permanent institution by House of Commons vote (17 July).

Deaths: H. Rider Haggard, author of *King Solomon's Mines* (14 May); Queen Alexandra, widow of King Edward VII (20 November).

1926

Birth of a daughter (later Elizabeth II) to the Duke and Duchess of York (later King George VI and Queen Elizabeth) (21 April).

Miners on strike (1 May–27 November); TUC called General Strike in support, which disrupted industry for nine days (3-13 May).

Canada associated as a member of the British Commonwealth of Nations.

The Earl of Halifax was made viceroy and governor-general of India.

British troops end occupation of the Rhineland.

Imperial Defence College for senior army, navy and air force officers
  founded.

Incorporation by Royal Charter of SSAFA—the Soldiers', Sailors'
  and Airmen's Families Association (founded 1885).

Legitimacy by marriage of parents made legal in England.

Reading University receives university status.

Publication of *A Drunk Man Looks at a Thistle* by Hugh MacDiarmid;
  of his memoir *The Seven Pillars of Wisdom* by T. E. Lawrence
  ('Lawrence of Arabia'); and of *Winnie the Pooh* by A. A. Milne.

Invention of television and first demonstration made by John Logie
  Baird (27 January).

First Grand Prix motor race held in Britain at Brooklands (7 August).

English Channel first swum by a woman, Gertrude Ederle (6 August).

1927

Allied military control of Germany ended.

Menin Gate, Belgium unveiled: memorial to the British who fell in
  the Ypres salient, World War I.

British Broadcasting Corporation (formerly British Broadcasting
  Company) constituted under Royal Charter (1 January).

First auomatic traffic lights set up (5 November).

Charles Wilson shared the Nobel Prize for physics.

First non-stop solo transatlantic flight made by Lindbergh.

First public demonstration of colour television in Glasgow.

Inauguration of the first automatic telephone service in London.
  Transatlantic telephone service began (7 January).

Initiation of the first radiotelephone service.

Champion Hurdle race at Cheltenham first run.

Greyhound racing began in Britain at White City (20 June).

Oxford and Cambridge Boat Race first broadcast (2 April).

Sir Malcolm Campbell became holder of world speed records on land
  and water.

Death of Jerome K. Jerome.

1928

Under terms of the Women's Suffrage Bill (7 May), women allowed
  to vote on the same basis as men (over twenty-one).

Kellog-Briand pact renouncing war signed in Paris by 65 states (27 August).

Formation of the World Association of Girl Guides and Girl Scouts.

Release of Oscar Slater after a campaign involving Conan Doyle and others against his wrongful imprisonment (for murder in 1909).

'Talkies' (moving pictures with sound) first shown in cinemas.

Institution of the Malvern Festival.

Publication of censored *Lady Chatterley's Lover* by D. H. Lawrence.

First transatlantic flight made by a woman, Amelia Earhart (New-foundland to Wales, 18 June).

Penicillin, the first antibiotic, discovered by Alexander Fleming of St Mary's Hospital, London.

Piccadilly Circus underground station opened in London.

First transmission of colour television made by John Logie Baird (3 July).

Deaths Thomas Hardy (11 January); Earl Haig (20 January); Herbert Asquith (15 February); Emmeline Pankhurst (14 June).

1929

General election (30 May): Labour minority government; Ramsay MacDonald became prime minister (until 1935).

Abolition of Poor Law system.

Foundation of St Peter's Hall, Oxford.

Margaret Bondfield became first woman privy councillor.

Courtauld Institute of Art established in London.

Ealing Studios established as Associated Talking Pictures.

Term 'documentary film' introduced.

The Daily Herald newspaper placed under the joint control of Odhams and the TUC.

The Listener weekly first published (16 January): publication ceased 1991.

Beginning of regional broadcasting with the opening of Brookmans Park transmitting station (21 October).

First experimental television broadcast by the BBC.

First trials held (14 October) of R101, the British dirigible designed by Barnes Wallis (16 December).

Frederick Hopkins shared the Nobel Prize for physiology or medicine.

The existence of a fifth dimension affirmed by Sir Owen Richardson.

Foundation of the Pony Club movement (1 November).
Deaths: the actress Lillie Langry (12 February); Lord Rosebery (21 May).

1930

Gandhi began his civil disobedience campagin against British rule in India (12 March).
  Publication of the Simon Report on India (24 June); Round Table Conference held in London on subject of India (12 November–19 January); Lord Willingdon became viceroy of India.
The independence of Iraq recognized by Britain (30 June).
Ratification of the London Naval Treaty between Britain, USA, France, Italy and Japan on naval disarmament.
Foundation of the Youth Hostels Association.
Unemployment reached two million.
Formation of the *News Chronicle* by the amalgamation of *The Daily News* and *The Daily Chronicle*.
John Masefield appointed poet laureate.
Amy Johnson became the first woman to fly solo from England to Australia (6–24 May).
R101 disaster: world's biggest airship exploded in France on maiden flight to India, killing 48 people (5 October).
Deaths: D. H. Lawrence (2 March); Arthur Balfour (19 March); Sir Arthur Conan Doyle (7 July).

1931

New Party founded by Sir Oswald Mosley along Facist lines (28 February).
Britain abandoned the gold standard (21 September) and devalued the pound.
Financial crisis led to coalition government under Ramsay MacDonald (25 August); Ramsay MacDonald replaced as leader of the Labour Party (28 August).
  General election (27 October): a second coalition national government formed under Ramsay MacDonald.
Statue of Westminster passed to regulate British Commonwealth relations (January); became law (11 December)
End of the civil disobedience campaign in India (March); Gandhi attended the second India Conference in London (1 December).

Mutiny over pay cuts at Invergordon naval base (15 September).

First publication of the Highway Code (14 April).

Foundation of the National Trust for Scotland for places of historic interest or natural beauty.

Reopening of Sadler's Wells Theatre, London (6 January).

The *New Statesman* absorbed *The Nation*.

King George V Dock, Glasgow, opened.

Death of Arnold Bennett (27 March).

1932

British Union of Fascists founded by Sir Oswald Mosley, replacing the New Party (December).

Irish election (16 February); Eamon de Valera elected prime minister of Ireland (9 March).

The Independent Labour Party under James Maxton seceded from the Labour Party.

Arrest of Gandhi in India (4 January)

Lausanne Pact between the Allies and Germany signed (July).

Foundation of the Methodist Church of Great Britain and Ireland, uniting the Wesleyan Methodist, Primitive Methodist and United Methodist Churches (20 September).

Opening of a new building for the Shakespeare Memorial Theatre in Stratford-on-Avon (23 April).

Publication of *Brave New World* by Aldous Huxley.

First experimental television programme broadcast by the BBC; Annual Christmas Day broadcast by the monarch instituted by George V; speech written by Rudyard Kipling.

First solo transatlantic flight by a woman when Amelia Earhart flew from Newfoundland to Londonderry (21 May).

Atomic nucleus split by Sir John Cockcroft and Dr Walton, releasing atom's energy.

Neutrons, nuclear particles, discovered by James Chadwick.

Piccadilly Circus lit by electricity for the first time.

Deaths: Edgar Wallace in Hollywood (10 February); Kenneth Grahame (6 July).

1933

Formation of the Popular Front, cooperation by leftwing parties against Fascism (until 1939).

rish elections (24 January); oath of allegiance removed from the
  constitution (May).
Codex Sinaiticus purchased from the Soviet government.
Discovery of the Tassili rock paintings by Lieutenant Brenans, an
  officer in the Camel Corps.
Foundation of the British Film Institute in London.
Discovery of polythene by ICI chemists.
Charter granted to the National Playing Fields Association.
Death of John Galsworthy (31 January).

1934

Formation of the Scottish Nationalist Party.
Civil disobedience campaign in India suspended by Gandhi (7 April).
Initiation of the Peace Pledge by the Rev. Dick Sheppard.
Opening of the Police Training College at Hendon (10 May).
The Iron Age fort of Maiden Castle, Dorset, excavated.
Glyndebourne Festival Opera founded by John Christie.
Publication of *I, Claudius* by Robert Graves and *Right Ho, Jeeves* by
  P. G. Wodehouse.
Official opening of the Mersey tunnel between Liverpool and
  Birkenhead (18 July, begun 16 December 1925).
Launch of the Atlantic passenger liner *Queen Mary* (26 September).
First women's cricket test match held in Australia (28 December).
Deaths: the composers Sir Edward Elgar (23 February), Gustav Holst
  (25 May) and Frederick Delius (10 June).

1935

Retirement of Ramsay MacDonald; Baldwin succeeded him as prime
  minister and formed a new National Government (7 June).
John Buchan became governor-general of Canada (until 1940).
Germany repudiated the Treaty of Versailles and accelerated rearma-
  ment programme.
Introduction of 30-mile speed limit in built-up areas (12 March) and
  of driving tests (1 June).
Alcoholics Anonymous (AA) founded.
Approval of (29 January) and implementation of (1 April) the Green
  Belt Scheme for London.
The first National Park in Britain started with a gift of 300 acres near
  Snowdon.

British Council established (chartered 1940).

First practical demonstration of radar by a team led by Robert
  Watson-Watt (26 February).

Death of T. E. Lawrence in a motor-cycle accident (19 May).

1936

Death of King George V from bronchitis (20 January): Edward VIII
  became king (January) and abidicated (10 December) to marry
  American divorcee Wallis Simpson. His brother, the Duke of York,
  became king as George VI (12 December).

Irish Republican Army proclaimed illegal (19 June).

Constitution of Orissa and Sind as separate Provinces of India (1 April).

Italy annexed Abyssinia: Haile Selassie lived in exile in England
  (until 1941) during the Italian occupation of Ethiopia.

End of the British protectorate of Egypt (ratified 22 December); the
  Anglo-Egyptian Treaty established an alliance allowing use of the
  Suez Canal for twenty years.

Opening of the first British open prison in, New Hall in Yorkshire (27
  May).

Jarrow 'hunger' march of unemployed people left Jarrow (5 October)
  and reached London (11 November).

Crystal Palace destroyed by fire (30 November).

Publication of *General Theory of Employment, Interest and Money* by
  John Maynard Keynes.

First television broadcast by the BBC (21 August); high-definition
  broadcast began (2 November).

Deaths: the writers Rudyard Kipling (18 January) and G. K. Chesteron
  (14 June).

1937

Marriage of the Duke of Windsor (formerly Edward VIII) and Mrs
  Wallis Simpson in France (3 June).

Neville Chamberlain became prime minster (until 1940) after the
  resignation of Stanley Baldwin (28 May).

Aden made Crown Colony.

Constitution of Punjab as an autonomous province.

Publication of a plan for the partition of Palestine (7 July).

Irish Free State renamed Eire (December).

Divorce for grounds other than adultery made legal in England.

Foundation of Nuffield College, Oxford, by Lord Nuffield.
Inter-Regional Spelling Competition became the first British quiz
  programme broadcast (25 November).
Lilliput periodical founded by Stefan Lorant.
First test-bed run of a jet engine developed by Frank Whittle.
The 999 telephone emergency service began (1 July).
Wimbledon lawn tennis championship first televised (21 June).
Deaths: Sir James Barrie (19 June); Lord Rutherford (19 October);
  Ramsay MacDonald (9 November).

1938

Signature of an agreement between Britain and Eire (25 April); last
  British troops depart (11 July).
Munich Pact made (29 September) between Neville Chamberlain, the
  French premier Daladier, Hitler and Mussolini appeased Hitler over
  Czechoslovakia: the fate of Sudetenland determined.
Singapore naval base opened (14 February); mobilization of the
  British fleet (27 September).
Wavell became commander in chief in the Middle East (until 1941).
Foundation of the Women's Voluntary Service (WVS) by the
  Marchioness of Reading (16 May); created Royal Women's
  Voluntary Service in 1966.
FA Cup final first televised (30 April).
Empire Exhibition held in Glasgow (May).
Coal industry taken over by the state.
Holidays with pay enforced by law.
The Iona Community founded by the Rev. George Macleod.
First publication of *Picture Post* periodical (ceased publication 1958).
Publication of *Brighton Rock* by Graham Greene.
Sir John Rothenstein became director of the Tate Gallery (until 1961).
Launch of the Atlantic passenger liner *Queen Elizabeth* (27 September).
Low-voltage fluorescent lighting available.

1939

George VI became first British monarch to visit North America.
Britain signed treaty of mutual assistance with Poland (24 March);
  denounced by Hitler (28 April).
Emergency Powers Bill (24 August) passed by parliament; conscription of men introduced (August, until 1960); evacuation of children

began; gas masks issued to civilians in Britain; Ministry of Information set up (abolished 1946).

World War II (ended 15 August 1945). *September*: Hitler invaded Poland (1); Britain and France declared war on Germany (3); British liner *Athenia* sunk off the Irish coast by a German submarine (4); first enemy air raid on Britain (6); British Expeditionary Force landed in France (11); Warsaw capitulated and Nazi-Soviet pact signed in Moscow for partitioning of Poland (29).

October: the *Royal Oak* torpedoed in Scapa Flow by German ships with the loss of 810 lives (14).

December: Battle of the River Plate (13-17 December): *Graf Spee*, German warship, scuttled in Montevideo harbour after being trapped by British cruisers. The *Graf Spee* was scuttled (17). Beginning of 'Phoney War' (ended March 1940).

Discovery of ship burial treasure at Sutton Hoo.

BBC Home Service began broadcasting (1 September).

Introduction of identity cards in Britain (30 September).

Deaths: the Irish poet playwright William Butler Yeats in France (28 January); Sigmund Freud, Austrian psychoanalyst, in London (23 September).

1940

World War II. *January*: introduction of food rationing (8, ended 1953). *February*: Battle of the Altmark (16).

April: Hitler invaded Denmark and Norway (9): British troops join fighting in Norway.

May: resignation of Neville Chamberlain as prime minister (10); Churchill became prime minister (11 May, until 1945) of a coalition National Government; British troops encircled on the French coast around Dunkirk (31); Home Guard founded as LDV (Local Defence Volunteers) (14), new name adopted July.

June: evacuation of British army from Dunkirk completed (4); Italy declared war on Britain and France (10); Paris captured by the Germans (14); France accepted terms for an armistice (22).

July: Channel Islands occupied by Germany (1); Battle of Britain began (10).

August: British Somaliland attacked by Italy (7); Britain began night bombing of Germany.

September: Blitz on London began; Battle of Britain ended in
victory (15); the George Cross and the George Medal instituted (23).
November: Greek troops repelled Iralian attacks; Coventry bombed
in worst air raid of the war, 1,000 killed; Coventry Cathedral (built
in the 15th century) destroyed (14, rebuilt 1954-62).
December: Sidi Barani captured by British troops in North Africa;
General Archibald Wavell began destruction of Italian forces in the
Western Desert; Germans dropped incendiary bombs on London.
Strips of metal first added to Bank of England £1 notes (29 March)
and ten-shilling notes (2 April) to make forgery more difficult.
Deaths: the author John Buchan, governor-general of Canada (11
February); Harold Harmsworth, Lord Rothermere, newspaper
baron; the physicist Sir Joseph John Thomson (30 August); Neville
Chamberlain (9 November).

1941

World War II. *January*: Tobruk taken by Commonweath troops (22).
February: Benghazi captured (7); Mogadishu in Somaliland
captured by Imperial troops (26); General Erwin Rommel's Afrika
Korps landed in Tripoli.
March: Lease-Lend (US aid to Britain programme, proposed 1940)
signed by President Roosevelt (11) (made reciprocal 1942); British
raid on Lofoten Islands off Norway (4); Italian fleet virtually
destroyed by British in Battle of Cape Matapan, off Crete (28);
Rommel began campaign in North Africa (30).
April: Benghazi captured by Rommel (3); Addis Ababa captured by
Imperial troops (4); Germans occupied Yugoslavia (17); Athens
captured by Germans (27); British and Commonwealth troops
landed in Crete; Ethiopia (conquered by Italy 1935-37) invaded by
British forces.
May: Rudolf Hess parachuted into Scotland (10); heavy German
bombing raid on London; destruction of the House of Commons
(11); Germans invaded Crete and British forces withdrew (20);
German battleship *Bismarck* sank HMS *Hood* (24); *Bismarck* sunk
(27).
June: clothes rationing began (2); Germany attacked Russia (20).
July: Syrian capital Damascus surrendered to Allied forces (21).
August: Atlantic Charter signed by Churchill and Roosevelt (11);

British and Russian troops attacked Iran (25); Syria occupied by
British and French (25).

September: in London General de Gaulle announced the formation
of a French provisional government in exile (25).

November: *Ark Royal* sunk by Italian torpedo (13); Eighth Army
began first offensive in Libya (18).

December: conscription of women in Britain (4, until 1947);
Japanese attacked Pearl Harbour (7); Britain and USA declared war
on Japan (8); Britain declared war on Finland, Romania and
Hungary (8); Japanese forces landed in Malaya (8); sinking of
Repulse and *Prince of Wales* (10); . Benghazi recaptured by British
(24); Hong Kong surrendered to Japanese (25).

First flight of the first British jet-propelled aircraft (15 May).

Bailey bridge invented by Donald Bailey.

First Outward Bound sea school opened at Aberdovey (autumn).

Deaths: Amy Johnson when she crashed into the Thames in the
cargo plane she was piloting for the Air Transport Auxiliary (5
January); Lord Robert Baden-Powell (8 January); James Joyce (13
January); the author Virginia Woolf by suicide (drowning) (28
March).

1942

World War II. *January*: Japanese forces landed in New Guinea and
Solomon Islands (23); German and Italian troops took Benghazi.

February: Introduction of soap rationing (9); Singapore fell to the
Japanese (15).

March: Java surrendered to the Japanese (9); German U-boat base at
St Nazaire attacked by British commandoes (27); RAF began
intensive bombing campaign against Germany (28).

April: George Cross awarded to the people of Malta (16).

May: Britain signed alliance with Russia (26); Rommel launched
offensive in Libya (27); 1,000 RAF bombers raided Cologne (31).

June: recapture of Tobruk by Rommel (20/21) following an eight-
month siege.

July: Sebastopol fell to the Germans (1); RAF made first daylight
raid on the Ruhr (16).

August: General Bernard Montgomery assumed command of the
Eighth Army (6); Allied raid on Dieppe (19); Battle of Alam el

Halfa (30): Rommel's attempt to break the Alamein Line to Cairo defeated by Eighth Army.

September: Madagascar fell to British forces (18); Eighth Army seized key German positions near El Alamein (30).

October: Battle of El Alamein (23-4 November): Allies victorious, Rommel in full retreat (30).

November: Allies invaded North Africa at Algiers, Casablanca and Oran (8); Benghazi recaptured by British (20).

ormation of the United Nations (organization established 1945).

everidge Plan published (20 November): scheme for national insurance devised by Lord Beveridge.

oundation of Oxfam (Oxford Committee for Famine Relief).

irst broadcast of Desert Island Discs (29 January).

irst discoveries made of the Mildenhall Treasure of Roman silver tableware near Mildenhall, Suffolk (continued into 1943).

943

World War II. *January*: Tripoli taken by the Eighth Army (23); Casablanca Conference of Allied powers (14-20): between Franklin Roosevelt and Churchill at which 'unconditional surrender' formula was agreed.

March: Battle of the Bismarck Sea (1–3/2-4); Rommel almost surrounded by US and British forces in North Africa (26).

May: remaining German and Italian forces surrendered to Allies in North Africa (12); RAF Dambuster raid on the Ruhr dams (17); Wavell appointed viceroy of India (18, until 1947).

July: Allied invasion of Sicily (10); Germans routed in Battle of Kursk (13); Mussolini overthrown (25).

August: Sicily fell to the Allies (17); Quebec Conference (11-24); Mountbatten appointed Supreme Allied Commander in South-East Asia (25).

September: Allies invaded Italian mainland (3); Italy surrendered (8); US forces landed at Salerno, near Naples (10); Germans occupied Rome (10); Smolensk taken by the Russians (25).

October: Naples fell to Allies (1); Russians crossed the Dneiper and captured Zaporozhie and Dnepropetrovsk (29).

November: Kiev taken by the Russians (6); Teheran Conference between Roosevelt, Stalin and Churchill (28).

December: General Dwight D. Eisenhower chosen as supreme
commander of Allied invasion of Europe (24); sinking of the German
battleship *Scharnhorst* off North Cape by the British Navy (26).
Nuffield Foundation formed by Lord Nuffield (13 February).
Sir John Barbirolli became conductor of the Halle Orchestra.
Deaths: Beatrice Webb, socialist and writer (30 April); the actor and
director Leslie Howard in a plane crash (1 June); Beatrice Potter,
children's author (22 December).

1944

World War II. *January*: Allied landings at Anzio Landings (22-25);
Russians raise German siege of Leningrad (19).
February: beginning of strategic bombing of Germany.
March: Monte Cassino destroyed by Allied bombing (15); Allied
force landed in Burma (19); General Orde Wingate killed in an air
crash.
April: General de Gaulle appointed head of the Free French Forces
(9); Russians drove Germans from the Crimea.
May: Monte Cassino fell to the Allies (18).
June: Allied forces entered Rome (4); Normandy Offensive
(codename Operation Overlord) began on D-Day: Allied troops
landed in Normandy (6); first V–1 rocket fell on England (18).
July: Caen fell to the Allies (9); Bomb Plot failed to kill Hitler (20).
August: Allied troops entered Florence (11); Allies landed in
southern France (15); Paris liberated (23); Romania declared war on
Germany (25).
September: Antwerp and Brussels taken by Allies (4); Boulogne
taken by Allies (7); Bulgaria declared war on Germany (7); V–2
rockets began to fall on England (8); Allies entered German soil
(11); Allied landings near Arnhem (17); Battle of Arnhem (19-28);
British troops landed in Greece (24).
October: British troops landed on mainland Greece (5); Rommel
committed suicide (14); Athens occupied by Allies (14); Aachen
taken by Allies (20); Red Army liberated Belgrade (20); Battle of
Leyte Gulf, Japanese sea power destroyed (25); Naval Battle of the
Philippines (23-25).
November: Home Guard disbanded (1); sinking of the German
warship *Tirpitz* by RAF bombs (12).

December: German counter-offensive in the Ardennes ('Battle of the Bulge') (16–22); Budapest surrounded by Red Army (26).

Education Act for England and Wales.

PAYE (Pay As You Earn) introduced in Britain by Sir Cornelius Gregg (6 April).

Pluto underwater oil pipeline from the Isle of Wight to France first in action (12 August).

Cancellation of the thirteenth official modern Olympic Games scheduled to be held in London.

Deaths: the architect Sir Edwin Lutyens; the conductor Sir Henry Wood (19 August); the humourist Heath Robinson (13 September).

1945

World War II. *January*: Warsaw captured by Russians (17); Hungary declared war on Germany (21); Red Army liberated Auschwitz (27).

February: Allied conference at Yalta (4); bombing of Dresden (14).

March: Cologne captured by Allies (6); Allies cross the Rhine (25).

April: Red Army entered Vienna (11); death of President Roosevelt (12); San Francisco Conference of the United Nations (25-26 June), charter signed (26); American troops and Red Army link up in Germany (27); Mussolini and his mistress show by Italian partisans (28); Allies penetrated Berlin (30); Hitler and his mistress committed suicide (30).

May: Germans surrendered in Italy (2); Berlin captured by Red Army (2); Rangoon fell to the British (3); war against Germany ended officially, Victory in Europe (VE Day) (8); naval air attacks on Japan (28).

June: arrest of William Joyce ('Lord Haw-Haw') for treason for broadcasting propaganda from Germany.

July: Polish government in Warsaw recognized by Allies (5); Labour won landslide in general election: Clement Atlee became prime minister (until 1951); Potsdam conference and Agreement (17 July-2 August).

August: atom bomb first used in warfare on Hiroshima (6) and Nagasaki (9); Russia declared war against Japan and advanced into Manchuria (8); unconditional surrender of Japan (14); VJ Day (15). Hong Kong re-occupied by British (30).

September: Second World War ends officially (2).

November: Nuremburg Trials began (20 November).
The United Nations came into existence formally 24 October.
Introduction of Family Allowance (15 June, later Child Benefit).
Publication of *Brideshead Revisited* by Evelyn Waugh.
Death of David Lloyd George (26 March).

1946

Bank of England nationalized (1 March).
Execution by hanging of William Joyce ('Lord Haw-Haw') for treason
  by broadcasting Nazi propaganda from Germany (3 January).
The term 'Iron Curtain' used in a speech by Sir Winston Churchill (5
  March) at Fulton, Missouri, to describe the barrier descending
  across Europe.
King David Hotel, British military HQ in Jerusalem, bombed by
  Jewish terrorists (22 July).
War Crimes Tribunal, World War II, at Nuremberg ended; executions
  carried out 16 October.
Ceylon gained independence.
Malacca incorporated in the Malayan Union.
British protectorate of Jordan ended and it became an independent
  kingdom.
Creation of the Royal Military Academy at Sandhurst by the combi-
  nation of Sandhurst and Woolwich (2 April).
Execution by hanging of Neville Heath for murder.
Introduction of television licences in Britain (1 June).
Formation of the Young Conservatives (6 July).
Introduction of bread rationing (22 July).
New Bodleian Library opened.
Thirty-three football fans crushed by collapsed barriers at Burnden
  Park in Bolton (9 March).
Premiere of *A Matter of Life and Death* by Michael Powell and
  Emeric Pressburger.
The Arts Council of Great Britain (formerly the Council for the
  Encouragement of Music and the Arts, founded 1940) incorporated.
ENIAC (Electronic Numerical Integrator and Calculator), first
  electronic computer, publicly demonstrated (February).
Deaths: the economist John Maynard Keynes (21 April); John Logie
  Baird (14 June); H. G. Wells (13 August).

1947

Coal industry nationalized (1 January).

GATT (General Agreement on Tariffs and Trade) signed by 23 nations.

The Marshall Plan for post-war recovery in Europe inaugurated by
George Marshall, US Secretary of State (22 September).

Marriage of Princess Elizabeth and Prince Philip, Duke of Edinburgh,
formerly Philip Mountbatten (20 November).

Lord Mountbatten appointed last viceroy of India to oversee the
transfer of power to the independent governments of India and
Pakistan (20 February).

India gained independence within the British Commonwealth and
separated into the separate dominions of Pakistan and India (15
August); Bengal and Punjab divided between India and Pakistan.

Burma proclaimed an independent republic (24 September); left the
British Commonwealth (17 October).

Groundnut scheme in Tanganyika began.

Foundation of St Benet's Hall, Oxford.

Raising of the school-leaving age to 15 (1 April).

The Edinburgh Festival of Music and Drama launched (24 August).

First British nuclear reactor built at Harwell.

First turboprop engine in use (in the Rolls-Royce Dart).

North Channel between Northern Ireland and Scotland first swum by
Tom Blower of Nottingham.

Deaths: the socialist and author Sidney Webb (13 October); Stanley
Baldwin, Earl Baldwin of Bewdley (14 December).

1948

Birth of Charles, Prince of Wales (14 November).

British Union of Fascists revived as British Union Movement by Sir
Oswald Mosley.

Plural voting discontinued by Act of Parliament.

The Independent Labour Party ceased to have parliamentary representation.

The Malayan Union became the Federation of Malaya.

Burma became independent and left the British Commonwealth (4
January).

Ceylon became a dominion within the British Commonwealth (4
February)

British mandate in Palestine ended; Palestine partitioned between Jordan and the new state of Israel (14 May).

Establishment of the Organization for European Economic Cooperation (OEEC) (16 April): superseded by the Organization for Economic Cooperation and Development (OECD) 1960.

Russian blockade of Berlin (18 June): Western airlift of supplies began.

British Railways inaugurated (1 January), amalgamating existing regional railway companies under national ownership.

Opening of the first supermarket in Britain, in London (12 January).

Bread rationing ended (29 July).

Electricity industry nationalized (1 April).

The National Health Service came into effect (5 July).

Alcoholics Anonymous founded in Britain (15 July).

Publication of *Nineteen Eighty-four* by George Orwell.

The Institute of Contemporary Arts founded in London.

Opening of the world's first port radar system at Gladstone Dock, Liverpool (30 July).

Production of the Morris Minor car, designed by Alex Issigonis, began (12 October).

Opening of the fourteenth official modern Olympic Games in London (29 July).

First British Grand Prix run at Silverstone (28 September).

Death of Sir Malcolm Campbell (31 December).

1949

Eire left the British Commonwealth (18 April).

Recognition of George VI as head of the Commonwealth (27 April).

North Atlantic Treaty signed in Washington DC (4 April, amended in London by protocol 17 October 1951), setting up the North Atlantic Treaty Organization (NATO), mutual defence pact between 12/13 European nations and the USA.

Council of Europe came into effect (5 May).

Berlin blockade lifted (6 October).

Test flight of the Canberra jet bomber (13 May).

Foundation of University College of North Staffordshire at Keele.

End of clothes rationing (15 March).

Nationalization of the gas industry (1 May).

First appearance of The Goon Show comedy series on BBC radio (ran until 1960).

Weather forecast first televised (29 July).

Publication of *1984* by George Orwell.

First flight of the Comet, the first jet-propelled airliner (27 July) and the Brabazon, the largest British aircraft (4 September).

The Nature Conservancy set up.

   Plans announced for twelve National Parks in England and Wales.

Death of the comedian Tommy Handley (9 January).

1950

Klaus Fuchs found guilty of betraying secrets of atomic bomb constructions to Russia (February).

Labour won general election, the first to be televised (24 February).

The Stone of Scone (Coronation Stone) stolen from Westminster Abbey by Scottish Nationalists (25 December, retrieved 1951).

India became a republic within the British Commonwealth (26 January).

Britain recognized Communist China.

Outbreak (June) of the Korean War between the United Nations and North Korea (ended June 1951): Britain sent troops (August).

Submarine HMS *Truculent* sunk in the Thames following a collision (12 January).

End of petrol rationing (26 May) and soap rationing (9 September).

Introduction of Legal Aid in Britain (2 October).

Foundation of St Anthony's College, Oxford.

The docking of horses' tails prohibited by law.

The Archers radio serial first broadcast by the BBC.

Nobel Prize for literature awarded to Bertrand Russell.

Publication of *The Lion, the Witch and the Wardrobe* by C. S. Lewis.

Link between cigarettes and lung cancer established.

The first gas turbine-powered car built by the Rover Company.

First Outward Bound mountain school opened in Eskdale.

The Peak District designated the first National Park in England (28 December).

Execution by hanging of Timothy Evans for the murder of his infant daughter while living in the house of John Christie; the charge of murdering his wife was not heard.

Deaths: George Orwell (21 January); Sir Harry Lauder (26 February);
  George Bernard Shaw (2 November).

1951

Stone of Scone found at Forfar (13 April).

British diplomats and spies, Guy Burgess and Donald Maclean,
  escape to the Soviet Union (26 May).

British troops seized Suez Canal Zone (19 October).

Winston Churchill became prime minister after Conservative victory
  in general election (25 October).

Cease-fire talks on the Korean War began (July): truce line established along the 28th parallel (November).

European Coal and Steel Community established by the Treaty of
  Paris (18 April).

Festival of Britain held (3 May-30 September).

Nationalization of railways (1 January).

First Miss World contest in London (19 April).

First party political broadcast on television, for the Lieral Party (15
  October).

Introduction of zebra pedestrian crossings (31 October).

First performance of the opera *Billy Budd* by Britten.

Deaths: the statesman Ernest Bevin (14 April); the actor and composer Ivor Novello (6 March).

1952

Death of King George VI (6 February): succession of his daughter as
  Elizabeth II.

Sovereignty of Ethiopia handed over by Britain.

State of Emergency declared in Kenya after series of Mau Mau
  terrorist killings.

Vincent Massey appointed as first Canadian governor-general of
  Canada (until 1959).

European Defence Community established (27 May).

Abolition of identity cards (21 February).

Lynmouth devastated by floods (16 August).

Minoan Script B form of Mycenaean Greek first deciphered by
  Michael Ventris.

Waiting for Godot by Samuel Beckett published.

First performance of *The Moustrap* by Agatha Christie (25 November).

Last tram ran in London (6 July).
Britain tested its first atomic bomb (3 October).
Myxomatosis introduced to destroy rabbits in Britain.

1953

Death of Queen Mary, widow of George V (24 March).
  Coronation of Queen Elizabeth II (2 June).
Mau Mau leader Jomo Kenyatta jailed in Kenya.
Nyasaland (now Malawi) federated with Southern and Northern
  Rhodesia to form the Federation of Rhodesia and Nyasaland (1
  August, until 1963).
Korean Truce formally ending the Korean War between the United
  Nations and North Korea signed (27 July).
End of sweet (4 February) and sugar rationing (26 September).
Amnesty granted to World War II deserters (23 February).
Execution of John Christie for murdering four women (15 July);
  Christie admitted to murdering six other women, including the wife
  of Timothy Evans.
Opening of the first television theatre, in Brighton.
First broadcast of the Panorama programme by BBC television (12
  November).
Sir Arthur Bliss made Master of the Queen's Musick.
Agreement signed for laying of the first transatlantic telephone cable.
The double helix structure of DNA (deoxyribonucleic acid) first
  identified by James D. Watson and Francis Crick.
Launch of the royal yacht *Britannia*.
Summit of Mount Everest reached (29 May) by Sir Edmund Hillary
  and Tenzing Norgay.
Deaths: the writer Hilaire Belloc (16 July); the contralto Kathleen
  Ferrier from cancer (8 October); the Welsh poet Dylan Thomas (9
  November).

1954

Anti-British rioting in Cyprus by supporters of EOKA (National
  Organization of Cypriot Combatants), demanding union with
  Greece.
Britain agreed to withdraw troops from the Suez Canal Zone (19
  October). Colonel Gamel Abdul Nasser seized power in Egypt
  (November).

End of food rationing in Britain (3 July).

Eurovision—first large-scale television link-up between European countries (6 June).

First broadcast and publication of *Under Milk Wood* by Dylan Thomas.

Publication of *Lord of the Flies* by William Golding and *Lucky Jim* by Kingsley Amis.

First four-minute mile run (6 May) by the medical student Roger Bannister.

Death by suicide of Alan Turing, inventor of the Turing Machine, who made important theoretical contributions to computer science.

1955

Sir Anthony Eden became prime minister (6 April, until 1957) after resignation of Churchill; general election (26 May) won by the Conservatives.

Clement Attlee resigned as Labour Party leader (7 December) and was replaced by Hugh Gaitskell.

Formal annexation by the Royal Navy of Rockall Island.

State of emergency declared in Cyprus after violent demonstrations against British rule.

Nationalization by Egypt of the Suez Canal. British evacuation of Suez Canal Zone.

Execution of Ruth Ellis by hanging for the murder of her lover (13 July): the last woman to be hanged in Britain.

Commercial television began in Britain (22 September).

Beginning of the exposure as a fraud of Piltdown man, discovered 1912 (21 November).

First experimental fast-breeder nuclear reactor started at Dounreay.

First gas turbine-powered ship (HMS *Grey Goose*).

Hetton oldest mineral railway line, Co. Durham (built by George Stephenson) closed.

Completion of the aircraft carrier HMS *Ark Royal* (25 February).

The hovercraft patented by its inventor, Christopher Cockerell (12 December).

Death of Sir Alexander Fleming (11 March).

1956

Jo Grimond became leader of the Liberal Party (until 1967).

Barbados and Jamaica became part of the British Caribbean Federation.

British deported Archbishop Makarios, leader of the Greek-Cypriot community, to the Seychelles (9 March).

Grant of a new constitution in Zanzibar.

Sudan became independent republic (1 January).

Suez Crisis: Britain evacuated Suez Canal Zone (18 June); Colonel Nasser, president of Egypt, seized the Suez Canal and nationalized it (26 July); Israel attacked Egypt (29 October); Anglo-French forces bombed Egyptian military targets (30 October); Allied forces retook Canal Zone (6 November); UN-imposed cease-fire (8 November); Canal blocked (16 November); British forces withdrawn after financial pressure from the US (23 November).

Abolition of third-class travel on British Railways (3 June).

ERNIE (Electronic Random Number Indicating Equipment) used to select winning numbers in Premiums Bonds, first issued for sale by the Department of National Savings (1 November).

Annual Kate Greenaway Medal award for illustration of children's books instituted in memory of Kate Greenaway.

First experimental transmission of colour television made from Alexandra Palace.

First performance of *Look Back in Anger* by John Osborne (May).

Commissioning of the first guided-missile ship (HMS *Girdle Ness*).

Official opening of Calder Hall atomic power station (17 October).

First Atlantic telephone cable opened for traffic.

Deaths: the Hungarian-born British film director Sir Alexander Korda (23 January); A. A. Milne, children's writer (31 January); the author and cartoonist Sir Max Beerbohm (20 May); the poet Walter de la Mare (22 June).

1957

Harold Macmillan became prime minister (until 1963) after resignation of Sir Anthony Eden (9 January).

The Gold Coast gained independence within the British Commonwealth as Ghana (6 March); British Togoland joined Ghana.

Establishment of the West Indies Federation (1 August).

Malaya became independent as a sovereign member state of the British Commonwealth (31 August, joined Malaysia 1963).

Euratom (European Atomic Energy Authority) established by Treaty of Rome (25 March).

European Economic Community established by Treaty of Rome (25
  March), made up of France, Germany, Italy and the Benelux nations.
Suez Canal reopened.
First British hydrogen bomb dropped over Christmas Island (15 May).
First Premium Bond draw by ERNIE (1 June).
Publication of *Room at the Top* by John Braine.
Truth magazine ceased publication.
Sputnik I (4 October) and Sputnik II (3 November) put into orbit
  round the earth.
Jodrell Bank radio telescope went into operation (11 October).
The entry into scheduled airline service of the first turboprop airliner
  (the Bristol Britannia).
The sedative drug Thalidomide first prescribed for pregnant women.
Death of the detective story writer Dorothy L. Sayers (18 December).

1958

Prince Charles created Prince of Wales by Queen Elizabeth II (26 July).
Women peers appointed to the House of Lords first took their seats
  (21 October).
EOKA terrorists step up campaign against British in Cyprus.
European Nuclear Energy Agency founded within OEEC (1 February).
The Yeomanry and Volunteer Force of the Territorial Army trans-
  ferred to the Territorial Force.
Campaign for Nuclear Disarmament (CND) founded by Bertrand
  Russell and Canon Collins (17 February); organized its first march
  from London to Aldermaston (7 April).
Opening of the Planetarium in London (21 March).
Presentation of the first Duke of Edinburgh Awards (4 June).
The last presentation of debutantes to the Queen (July).
Introduction of parking meters in Westminster, London (July).
The Litter Act came into force (7 August).
Race riots in the Notting Hill Gate area of London and in Nottingham
  (September).
First performance of *The Birthday Party* by Harold Pinter.
Publication of *Picture Post* ceased.
Award of the Nobel Prize for chemistry to Frederick Sanger.
Development and manufacture of the hovercraft, invented by Christopher
  Cockerell, undertaken.

Entry into airline service of the first turbojet (the De Havilland Comet).

First heart pacemaker inserted.

First oil tanker of 100,000 deadweight tonnage built.

Opening of Gatwick Airport (9 June).

Opening by Harold Macmillan of the first motorway in Britain, the Preston bypass (5 December).

Thalidomide drug implicated in birth defects (December).

First drive-in bank in Britain opened in Liverpool (January).

Dr Vivian Fuchs completed first overland crossing of Antarctica.

Empire Games were held in Cardiff (July).

Seven members of Manchester United football team killed in a plane crash at Munich airport (6 February).

Deaths: Dame Christabel Pankhurst (13 February); the actors Ronald Colman (19 May) and Robert Donat (9 June); the composer Ralph Vaughan Williams (16 August); the pioneer of family planning, Marie Stopes (2 October); the shipping magnate and art collector Sir William Burrell.

1959

Conservatives under Harold Macmillan won general election (8 October).

Agreement by Greece, Turkey and Britain on Cyprus (February)

Singapore became an independent state within the British Commonwealth (3 June).

European Free Trade Association (EFTA) inaugurated as a rival trading bloc to European Economic Community (3 May).

Last fly-past of Hurricane bombers and Spitfire fighters over London to commemorate the Battle of Britain (20 September).

Introduction of the postcode in Britain (3 October).

Main section of the Ml motorway from London to Birmingham officially opened (2 November).

Empire Day became Commonwealth Day (24 May).

Hugh Carleton Greene became director-general of the BBC (until 1969).

The Mermaid Theatre became the first English theatre to be opened in the City of London since the Restoration (28 May).

Opening of Chapelcross nuclear power station in Dumfriesshire (2 May).

First Dover-Calais crossing by hovercraft (25 July).

Introduction of telephone trunk call dialling in Britain (5 September).

Launch of the *Oriana*, the first transverse-propelled ship.

Maiden voyage made of the British *Auris*, the world's first gas turbine-powered oil tanker.

The first heliport in Britain opened in London (23 April).

British Motor Corporation launched the Mini (August).

Loch Lomond first swum by Commander Gerald Forsberg, a distance of 22 miles.

Deaths: the sculptor Sir Jacob Epstein (21 August); the painter Sir Stanley Spencer.

1960

'Wind of Change' speech by Harold Macmillan to the South African Parliament in Cape Town (3 February).

Sharpeville Massacre in South Africa (21 March): 56 Africans killed by police.

Somalia united with the British Somaliland to become the Somali Republic (1 July).

The Gold Coast and British Togoland (united in 1957) became the independent republic of Ghana within the British Commonwealth (1 July).

British rule ended and Cyprus became an independent republic (16 August): Archbishop Makarios elected as the first president of the new republic.

Nigeria became an independent country within the British Commonwealth (1 October).

Launch of the *Dreadnought*, Britain's first nuclear-powered submarine (21 October).

Marriage of Princess Margaret and Antony Armstrong-Jones (later Lord Snowdon) (6 May).

Churchill College, Cambridge, opened.

Mumbles Railway, Swansea, the oldest British passenger railway closed (1 January).

Introduction of MOT (Ministry of Transport) tests on motor vehicles (12 September).

Introduction of traffic wardens in London (15 September).

Foundation of the Royal Shakespeare Company.

News Chronicle incorporated in *The Daily Mail.*

Publication of the complete *Lady Chatterley's* Lover by D. H.

Lawrence (2 November): 'Lady Chatterley' trial in London:
Penguin Books found not guilty of publishing obscene material.
Coronation Street first shown on television (9 December).
First proposal of SI units (Système International) as internationally
accepted standard of scientific units: metre, kilogram, second,
ampere, kelvin, mole and candela.
Nobel Prize for physiology or medicine awarded to Sir Peter Medawar
and Sir Frank Burnet for work on immunological tolerance.
English Football League matches first televised (10 September).
Deaths: English-born Australian writer Nevil Shute (12 January);
statesman Aneurin Bevan (6 July); the suffragette Sylvia Pankhurst.

1961

British police arrested members of the Portland spy ring (January).
Jamaica left the West Indies Federation (19 September).
Northern Cameroons joined the Federation of Nigeria (1 June). Sierra
Leone (27 April) and Tanganyika (9 December) became independ-
ent within the British Commonwealth. Union of South Africa
withdrew from the Commonwealth (15 March) and became a
republic (31 May). Kuwait became completely independent.
The Organization for Economic Cooperation and Development
(OECD) established in Paris (30 September), succeeded the
Organization for European Economic Cooperation (OEEC).
Amnesty International founded.
The farthing ceased to be legal tender in Britain (1 January).
The Pill, oral contraceptive, went on sale in Britain.
Introduction of mini cabs in London (6 March).
Black-and-white £5 notes issued by the Bank of England ceased to be
legal tender (13 March).
Opening of betting shops (1 May).
Enthronement of Dr Ramsey as hundredth archbishop of Canterbury
(27 June).
First performance of the review *Beyond the Fringe* at the Edinburgh
Festival with Alan Bennett, Peter Cook, Jonathan Miller and Dudley
Moore.
Completion of the Tamar Bridge linking Cornwall and Devon.
Deaths: the conductor Sir Thomas Beecham (8 March); the painter
Augustus John (31 October); the comedian George Formby.

1962

Western Samoa became independent within the Commonwealth (1
January). Dissolution of the West Indies Federation (31 May):
Jamaica (5 August) and Trinidad and Tobago (31 August) became
independent within the Commonwealth. Uganda became independent within the Commonwealth (9 October); Tanganyika became a
republic within the Commonwealth (9 December).

Consecration of Coventry Cathedral (15 May, begun 1951), designed by
Basil Spence.

Establishment of the National Theatre in London with Sir Laurence
Olivier as director (9 August).

Nobel Prize for medicine and physiology awarded to Francis Crick
and James D. Watson for their double-helix model of the structure
of DNA.

Telstar communications satellite launched (10 July): first live
transatlantic television broadcast.

Thalidomide withdrawn from the market after discovery that it caused
severe birth defects.

World's first passenger hovercraft entered service.

Deaths: the historian Richard Tawney; the writer Victoria Sackville-
West; the historian George Trevelyan (21 July); the actor Charles
Laughton (15 December).

1963

Defection of Kim Philby to the Soviet Union (January).

Unexpected death of Gaitskell, leader of the Labour Party (18
January): succeeded by Harold Wilson (14 February).

The Profumo Affair: resignation (5 June) of John Profumo, Secretary
of State for War, after lying to Parliament about an affair with a call
girl, Christine Keeler, who was also involved with a Russian
diplomat.

The Profumo Affair and ill health forced Macmillan to retire (10
October); succeeded by Sir Alec Douglas-Home, formerly Lord
Home (30 November).

Aden joined the South Arabian Federation (21 March). Formation of
the Federation of Malaysia (16 September): made up of Malaya,
Singapore, Sabah and Sarawak. Nigeria became a republic (1
October) within the British Commonwealth. British protectorate of

Zanzibar ended and it became independent (9 December). Kenya gained independence within the British Commonwealth (12 December).

Violent clashes between Turkish and Greek Cypriots in Cyprus: UN peace forces intervened (22 December).

President de Gaulle of France vetoed British entry into the European Economic Community (29 January).

Test Ban Treaty signed by Britain, US and Russia (5 August).

Britain agreed to buy Polaris missiles from the US.

Beeching Report recommended extensive cuts in British railway branch lines (27 March).

Great Train Robbery (8 August): £2.5 million stolen from the Glasgow to London mail train (12 of the gang were tried and convicted 1964).

Doctor Who, children's TV series, began.

Publication of *The Spy Who Came in from the Cold* by John Le Carré.

The Beatles pop group founded (disbanded 1970).

Opening of the Dartford Tunnel under the Thames (18 November).

Deaths: the motor car manufacturer and philanthropist Lord Nuffield (22 August); the writer Aldous Huxley (22 November).

1964

Harold Wilson became prime minister (until 1970) after a general election (15 October).

Zanzibar became a republic (12 January) and joined Tanganyika to form the United Republic of Tanzania (27 April). Southern Rhodesia renamed Rhodesia (until 1979); Ian Smith became prime minister (8 April). Nyasaland (now Malawi) became independent within the Commonwealth (6 July). Malta became independent (21 September). Northern Rhodesia became the independent republic of Zambia within the British Commonwealth (24 October). Kenya became a republic within the Commonwealth (12 December).

Last hangings in Britain (13 August): Peter Allen and John Walby.

First broadcast of Radio Caroline radio station (28 March) and of the BBC2 television channel (21 April). Opening of Radio Manx, first British commercial radio station (23 November).

Official opening of the Forth Road Bridge (4 September, begun 21 November 1958).

Blue Streak, first British rocket launched into space at Woomera, Australia (5 June).

World land speed record set by Donald Campbell in Australia (17 July).

Deaths: Lord Beaverbrook, Canadian-born British newspaper tycoon (9 June); the novelist Ian Fleming, creator of James Bond (12 August).

1965

Resignation of Sir Alec Douglas-Home as leader of the Conservative Party: Edward Heath became its first elected leader.

The Gambia gained independence as a kingdom within the British Commonwealth (18 February). The Maldives in the Indian Ocean became independent (26 July). Singapore separated from Malaysia (9 August). Rhodesia declared unilateral declaration of independence (UDI) (11 November); Ian Smith's regime declared illegal.

Free-trade pact between Britain and Eire (14 December).

Opening of the Pennine Way from Derbyshire to Roxburghshire (23 April).

Abolition of the death penalty for murder (9 November).

Formation of the Greater London Council (1 April).

Television advertising of cigarettes banned (31 July).

Opening of the Post Office Tower, tallest building in Britain (7 October).

Introduction of a speed limit of 70 miles per hour on motorways (22 December).

Confederation of British Industries (CBI) founded.

Starting stalls first used in horse races, at Newmarket (8 July).

Deaths: the American-born British poet T. S. Eliot (4 January); Sir Winston Churchill (24 January); the British-born American comedian Stan Laurel (23 February).

1966

General election (31 March): Labour won.

The first Welsh Nationalist member of parliament, Gwynfor Evans, took his seat (21 July) after a by-election.

Opening of Parliament first televised (21 April).

Bechuanaland became fully independent as Botswana (30 September). British protectorate ended and Basutoland (now Lesotho) became independent (4 October). British Guiana became the independent republic of Guyana within the Commonwealth. Barbados became independent within the Commonwealth (30 November).

Aberfan disaster in Wales (27 October): 144 people killed, including
116 children, by a collapsing slag heap.

Moors murders Myra Hindley and Ian Brady sentenced to life
imprisonment (6 May).

Special Christmas stamps issued for the first time (1 December).

First performance of *Rosencrantz and Guildenstern are Dead* by Tom
Stoppard.

Official opening of the Severn Bridge (8 September).

Launch of Britain's first Polaris submarine, *Resolution* (16 September).

Discovery of gas fields in the North Sea (May).

The first non-stop solo voyage around the world begun by Francis
Chichester (27 August).

The first Britons to row across the Atlantic, Captain John Ridgway
and Sergeant Chay Blyth, arrived 3 September.

World Cup held in England: won by the England team (30 July).

Death of the novelist Evelyn Waugh (10 April).

1967

Abortion Bill passed by parliament (25 October).

Jeremy Thorpe elected leader of the Liberal Party after the retirement
of Jo Grimond (18 January).

Colony status of Antigua ended. Uganda became a republic (8
September). Last British troops left Aden (30 November); Aden
became part of People's Republic of Southern Yemen. St Lucia
gained self-government.

The first Scottish Nationalist member of parliament, Winifred Ewing,
took her seat (2 November) after a by-election.

Britain reapplied to join the European Economic Community.

Renationalization of the steel industry (28 July).

Introduction of majority jury verdicts in English courts; first instance
in Brighton (5 October).

Introduction of breathalyser tests (8 October).

First British ombudsman, Sir Edmund Compton, took office (1 April).

Opening of the Roman Catholic Cathedral in Liverpool (14 May).

Colour television first broadcast by BBC2 (1 July).

Radio 1 first broadcast by the BBC (30 September).

Opening of the first local radio station, Radio Leicester (8 November).

North Sea gas first pumped ashore in Co. Durham (4 March).

The oil tanker Torrey Canyon went aground off Land's End causing
major pollution of the coastline (30 March).
Launch of the first British satellite, Ariel III (5 May).
Cunard liner *Queen Elizabeth II* launched by Queen Elizabeth II (20
September).
The first non-stop solo voyage around the world completed by
Francis Chichester (28 May): he was knighted by Elizabeth II.
Brian Epstein, manager of the Beatles, committed suicide.
Death of Donald Campbell, killed in jet-powered boat *Bluebird* crash
on Lake Coniston attempting to break the world water-speed record
(4 January).
Death of the poet laureate John Masefield (12 May); Cecil Day Lewis
became poet laureate.
Deaths: Sir Victor Gollancz, founder of the Left Book Club (8 February);
the actress Vivian Leigh (8 July);the poet Siegfried Sassoon (1
September); Clement Attlee (8 October); the writer Arthur Ransome.
Murder of the playwright Joe Orton by his lover, Kenneth Halliwell,
who committed suicide.

1968

Enoch Powell made his 'rivers of blood' speech on immigration (6 May).
Race Relations Act came into force (26 November).
Mauritius became an independent within the British Commonwealth
(12 March). Swaziland became independent as a kingdom within
the British Commonwealth (6 September).
Collapse after a gas explosion of the high-rise building Ronan Point,
killing three people.
Introduction of breath tests to monitor the level of alchohol in the
blood of drivers.
Introduction of two levels of postal service, first and second class (16
September).
Issue of 5p and 10p decimal coins (23 April).
Opening of the University of Ulster at Coleraine, Northern Ireland (1
October).
Violent anti-Vietnam war demonstrations in London (17 March).
Publication of *2001, A Space Odyssey* by Arthur C. Clarke.
Opening of the new Euston Station (14 October).
The first heart transplant operation in Britain was carried out (3 May).

MCC tour of South Africa cancelled by the South African prime minister, John Vorster, because of the presence in the English team of the player Basil D'Oliviera.

European Cup first won by an English team, Manchester United (29 May).

Deaths: the racing driver Jim Clark in a crash during the German Grand Prix (7 April); the comedian Tony Hancock in Australia by suicide (24 June); the children's writer Enid Blyton (28 November).

1969

Investiture of Prince Charles as Prince of Wales at Caernarvon Castle (1 July).

Northern Ireland Crisis. Eruption of violence between Protestant and Catholic communities in Northern Ireland: British troops were sent to suppress conflict (August); a 'peace wall' was constructed between the two communities in Belfast (28 September); the formation of the Ulster Defence Regiment was agreed by Parliament (18 December).

Formation of St Vincent and the Grenadines into a British Associated State (until 1979).

Voting age lowered from 21 to 18 (17 April).

Television broadcasting in colour began (14 November).

Introduction of the 50p decimal coin (14 October).

Abolition of the death penalty for murder (18 December).

British-built supersonic *Concorde* made maiden flight (9 January).

Oil discovered in the British and Norwegian sectors of the North Sea.

Deaths: the rock musician Brian Jones, of the Rolling Stones; the children's writer Richmal Crompton, creator of William.

1970

Northern Ireland Crisis. Riots in the Catholic Bogside district of Londonderry; troops sealed if off (29 March); first use of rubber bullets by the army in Belfast (2 August); Democratic Unionist Rev. Ian Paisley became a Stormont (April) and Westminster member of parliament (June); foundation of the liberal Alliance Party (April); the Social Democratic and Labour Party (SDLP) launched by Gerry Fitt and John Hume as a moderate nationalist party (21 August).

Conservatives won general election (19 June) and Edward Heath became prime minister (until 1974).

Britain made third application to join European Economic Community.

Guyana became a republic (23 February).

Rhodesia proclaimed a republic (2 March).

Tonga (4 June) and Fiji (10 October) gained independence within the British Commonwealth.

High Court award of damages to children with birth defects caused by the drug Thalidomide (23 March).

Decimal postage stamps first issued for sale in Britain (17 June).

The ten-shilling banknote went out of circulation (20 November).

Publication of *The Female Eunuch* by Germaine Greer.

Split of The Beatles pop group (April).

Return of the *Great Britain* to Bristol from the Falklands (23 June).

Deaths: the philosopher Bertrand Russell (2 February); the novelist E. M. Forster (7 June); the Conservative politician Ian MacLeod (20 July); the conductor Sir John Barbirolli (29 July).

1971

Introduction of decimal currency in Britain (15 February).

Northern Ireland Crisis. James Chichester-Clark resigned as prime minister of Northern Ireland and was succeeded by Brian Faulkner (21 March); Britain sent more troops and introduced internment (imprisonment without trial) to combat IRA terrorism (August).

Agreement signed to prepare Rhodesia's legal independence from Britain and settle issue of transistion to African majority rule.

Declaration of Sierra Leone as a republic.

East Bengal fought war of independence and became Bangladesh.

Bahrain (British protectorate from 1861) and the Persian Gulf State of Qatar became independent.

Open University inaugurated.

Sixty-six football fans crushed by collapsed barrier at Ibrox Park stadium in Glasgow (2 January).

1972

Northern Ireland Crisis. Bloody Sunday, Londonderry, Northern Ireland (30 January): British paratroopers fired on civil rights demonstrators, killing thirteen. Parliament of Northern Ireland suspended and replaced by direct rule from London.

Ceylon became a republic within the British Commonwealth and renamed Democratic Socialist Republic of Sri Lanka (22 May).

Idi Amin expelled 50,000 Ugandan Asians with British passports.

Nobel Peace prize awarded to Amnesty International.

Death of the poet laureate and novelist Cecil Day Lewis (22 May);
  Sir John Betjeman appointed poet laureate (10 October).

Death of the Duke of Windsor (formerly Edward VIII) in Paris (28 May).

1973

Britain and Ireland joined the European Economic Community (the
  Common Market) (1 January).

Miners' strike brought government announcement of three-day week
  to conserve fuel stocks (13 December).

Bahamas became independent country within the British Commonwealth (10 July).British Honduras ren amed Belize.

First woman allowed on to the floor of the London Stock Exchange
  (26 March).

VAT (Value-Added Tax) introduced in Britain (1 April).

British Library established.

Introduction of teletext for displaying information on a TV screen.

First commercial radio station (London Broadcasting) began transmission (8 October).

Red Rum was winner of the Grand National (31 March).

Deaths: the playwright Sir Noel Coward (26 March); the writer John
  Ronald Reuel Tolkein (2 September); the poet W. H. Auden (28
  September).

1974

Edward Heath resigned, and Harold Wilson led minority government
  after snap election (March); Labour won second election with tiny
  majority (October); Wilson prime minister until 1976.

IRA bombs killed 21 and injured 120 in two Birmingham pubs.

Grenada became fully independent within the Commonwealth (7
  February).

Disappearance of Lord Lucan after the murder of his children's nanny
  and the attempted murder of his wife (7 November).

Covent Garden fruit market moved to Nine Elms (8 November).

First large-scale prototype fast-breeder nuclear reactor at Dounreay.

Death of the writer Eric Linklater.

1975

Internment (detention without trial) ended in Northern Ireland.

Margaret Thatcher elected first woman leader of the Conservative Party.

Referendum held on Britain's entry to the European Community (5
   June); result in favour of staying in the Community.
First live broadcast of House of Commons debate.
Introduction of the first domestic video recorders (Sony Betamax).
The Equal Pay Act and the Sex Discrimination Act came into effect
   (27 December).
Dr Donald Coggan became archbishop of Canterbury (25 January).
Rev. David Sheppard became bishop of Liverpool.
North Sea oil first pumped ashore in Britain (11 June).
Deaths: Sir Pelham Grenville Wodehouse (14 February); Sir Arthur
   Bliss, Master of the Queen's Musick (27 March); racing driver Graham
   Hill in a plane crash (29 November); the scientist and philosopher Sir
   Julian Huxley; Neville Cardus, music critic and cricket writer.

1976

Harold Wilson resigned: succeeded as prime minister by James
   Callaghan (until 1979).
Jeremy Thorpe resigned as leader of the Liberal Party; David Steel
   elected to replace him.
Ian Smith accepted British proposal for majority rule in Rhodesia,
   ending eleven years of illegal independence.
Seychelles became an independent republic within the Common-
   wealth (28 June).
Opening of the National Exhibition Centre at Birmingham by
   Elizabeth II (2 February).
Publication of *The Selfish Gene* by Richard Dawkins.
First scheduled supersonic passenger service inaugurated: two
   Concorde airliners took off simultaneously from London and Paris
   (21 January).
Deaths: the crime writer Dame Agatha Christie (12 January); the
   artist Laurence Stephen Lowry (23 February); the commander Field
   Marshal Bernard Law Montgomery, Viscount Montgomery of El
   Alamein (24 March); the composer Benjamin Britten (4 December).

1977

Liberal and Labour parties form Lib-Lab Pact.
Award of the Nobel Prize for chemistry to Frederick Sanger.
Red Rum won the Grand National for the third time, a record (2 April).
Deaths: the actor Peter Finch (14 January); the playwright Terence

Rattigan (30 November); the film actor and director Sir Charles
Chaplin (25 December).

1978

Beginning of 'Winter of Discontent', a time of pay freezes and strikes
under the Callaghan Labour government.
Ecu international currency unit adopted by the European Community.
The *in vitro* fertilization technique first used successfully: first 'test-
tube baby', Louise Browne, born (25 July).

1979

General election: Labour defeated. Margaret Thatcher became first
British woman prime minister (4 May, until 1990).
Nationalist hopes for devolution killed by referendum results: a
majority vote against a Welsh Assembly, and only 33 per cent for a
Scottish Assembly, short of the 40 per cent required.
Lancaster House agreement arranged ceasefire in the guerrilla war in
Rhodesia and elections to effect transfer to Black majority rule in a
new state to be called Zimbabwe.
St Lucia and St Vincent gained full independence within the Com-
monwealth.
Robert Runcie became archbishop of Canterbury (until 1990).
Earl Mountbatten of Burma murdered by an IRA bomb (27 August).
Sir Anthony Blunt, Surveyor of the Queen's Pictures, revealed as
Soviet spy, the 'fourth man' in the Burgess, Maclean and Philby
affair; stripped of his knighthood.
Death of the actress and singer Dame Gracie Fields (27 September).

1980

Michael Foot succeeded James Callaghan as Labour Party leader.
Rhodesia gained independence as Zimbabwe.
SAS stormed Iranian embassy in London to release hostages held by
terrorists.
British Telecom (BT) created when the telephone service split from
the Post Office (privatized as a public limited company 1984).
Jeremy Thorpe, former leader of the Liberal Party, acquitted in
conspiracy trial.
John Lennon assassinated in New York (8 December).
Modernized Book of Common Prayer published.
Publication of *Rites of Passage* by William Golding.

Deaths: film director Sir Alfred Hitchcock (29 April); actor and
comedian Peter Sellers (24 July); Sir Oswald Mosley in France (3
December); the naturalist Joy Adamson; the photographer and
designer Sir Cecil Beaton.

1981

Hunger strike by IRA prisoners at the Maze Prison in Northern
Ireland: ten died.

The Social Democratic Party (SDP) founded by the 'gang of four', four
defectors from the Labour Party: David Owen, Shirley Williams, Roy
Jenkins and William Rodgers.

Belize became independent 21 September. Independence of Bechuanaland as Botswana. Independent state of Antigua and Barbuda set up.

Peter Sutcliffe convicted of Yorkshire Ripper murders.

Prince Charles married Lady Diana Spencer in St Paul's Cathedral:
700 million watched on television worldwide (29 July).

Rioting in Brixton, Liverpool and Manchester in response to
allegedly heavy policing.

Official opening of the Humber Estuary Bridge (17 July).

Deaths: the actress and singer Jessie Matthews; the football manager
Bill Shankly (29 September).

1982

Birth of a son, Prince William, to the Prince and Princess of Wales
(21 June).

Argentina invaded the Falkland Islands in the South Atlantic (British
Crown Colony since 1833) (2 April); Margaret Thatcher sent Task
Force (5 April); Argentine cruiser *General Belgrano* sunk by
torpedoes (2 May); HMS *Sheffield* hit by Exocet missile (4 May);
first land battles between Argentinian and British troops (21 May);
Argentine attack on two British supply ships off Bluff Cove (7
June); Argentinians surrendered (14 June).

Raising of the *Mary Rose* from the Solent (11 October, sank 1545).

Unemployment in Britain reached over three million.

Women's Peace Camp established at Greenham Common in Berkshire to protest against planned siting of US Cruise missiles at
nearby US military base.

First visit to Britain of a reigning pope: arrival of John Paul II (28 May).

Britain's fourth television channel, Channel Four, went on the air.

Thames flood barrier raised for the first time.

1983

Margaret Thatcher re-elected in landslide general election.

Neil Kinnock elected leader of the Labour Party.

Brunei achieved independence.

US troops invaded Grenada to remove Cuban presence from the island.

The wearing of front seat-belts in cars made compulsory (31 January).

'Hitler Diaries' exposed as fake after extracts published in the
  German news magazine *Stern* and *The Sunday Times*.

The Nobel Prize for literature awarded to William Golding, author of
  The Lord of the Flies.

Deaths: the Hungarian-born British writer Arthur Koestler and his wife
  by suicide; actors David Niven and Sir Ralph Richardson; author
  Dame Rebecca West; composer Sir William Walton (8 March).

1984

European Union established by treaty (February).

Bomb attack by the IRA on a Brighton hotel used by Conservative
  politicans during the Party Conference (12 October): five killed.

Diplomatic ties with Libya severed after the shooting of WPC Yvonne
  Fletcher outside the Libyan embassy in London.

BBC TV report on the famine in Ethiopia prompted massive aid effort.

Miners' national strike against pit closures began.

York Minster badly damaged by fire (9 July).

HIV (human immuno-deficiency virus) discovered as cause of Aids.

Death of the poet laureate Sir John Betjeman (19 May). Ted Hughes
  became poet laureate.

Deaths: Sir Arthur Travis ('Bomber') Harris, British commander of
  the RAF during World War II; actors James Mason and Richard
  Burton; the actress Diana Dors; the comedian Eric Morecambe; the
  playwright J. B. Priestley.

1985

House of Lords proceedings televised for the first time.

Miners voted to end year-long national strike.

Wreckage of the *Titanic* located 550 miles south of Newfoundland
  (September): explored July 1986.

Live Aid Concert raised £40 million in aid for famine victims in
  Ethiopia.

Summit of Everest reached by Chris Bonington.

British football teams banned indefinitely from European competition after 38 people died as Liverpool fans rioted at Heysel Stadium, Brussels.

Deaths: the actor Sir Michael Redgrave; the fashion designer Laura Ashley; the journalist and author James Cameron; the poets Robert Graves and Philip Larkin.

1986

Cabinet ministers Michael Heseltine and Leon Brittain resigned over the Westland Affair.

Jeffrey Archer resigned as chairman of the Conservative Party after allegations of payments to a prostitute.

Single European Act signed (February).

Appearance of Halley's Comet (named after Edmund Halley).

Construction of the Channel Tunnel began.

Deaths: Cary Grant, British-born American actor; the sculptor Henry Moore.

1987

Princess Anne created Princess Royal.

General election (14 June): Margaret Thatcher re-elected for third term as prime minister.

Government announced plans to introduce the Community Charge, a poll tax to replace the rates system for funding local services.

David Owen resigned as leader of the SDP in opposition to talks about merging with the Liberals.

IRA bomb killed eleven people at Remembrance Day service in Enniskillen, Northern Ireland (8 November).

Terry Waite, special envoy of the archbishop of Canterbury, kidnapped in Beirut by members of the militant Islamic group Hezbollah.

The car ferry *Herald of Free Enterprise* capsized off Zeebrugge with the loss of 188 lives.

The Order of the Garter opened to women.

'Black Monday' in the City of London: over £100 billion wiped off the value of shares on the stock market.

Death from multiple sclerosis of the cellist Jacqueline du Pre.

1988

Copyright Act.

Merger of the Liberal Party and the Social Democratic Party to form
the Social and Liberal Democratic Party (SDLP).

Lockerbie Disaster: a terrorist bomb destroyed Pan Am flight 103,
which crashed on to a Scottish village killing 244 passengers, 15
crew and 11 on the ground (21 December).

Piper Alpha disaster: 167 workers killed by explosion on an oil rig in
the North Sea.

The National Theatre became the Royal National Theatre.

Publication of *A Brief History of Time* by Stephen Hawking.

Deaths: the actor Trevor Howard; the choreographer Sir Frederick
Ashton; the comedy actor Kenneth Williams.

1989

Nigel Lawson, Chancellor of the Exchequer, resigned from the
government over differences on economic policy.

Poll tax implemented as Community Charge in Scotland.

Privatization of water authorities in England.

Guildford Four (Gerard Conlon, Carole Richardson, Patrick
Armstrong and Paul Hill) convicted of IRA pub bombings in 1974,
based on confessions fabricated by the police, are released.

Hillsborough Stadium disaster in Sheffield (15 April): 95 football
fans crushed to death at Liverpool vs Nottingham Forest match.

House of Commons proceedings first televised. Satellite television
began in Britain.

Fatwa (order to kill) instituted by Ayatollah Khomeni against the
author Salman Rushdie for supposedly blasphemous content of his
novel *Satanic Verses*: Rusdie went into hiding.

Deaths: the actor Lord Olivier; the novelist Daphne du Maurier; the
philosopher A. J. Ayer; the psychiatrist R. D. Laing.

1990

Britain joined the ERM (Exchange Rate Mechanism) for the stabilization
of currency in the European Monetary System (October).

Britain rejected timetable for a single European currency by the year
2000 at EC summit in Rome.

Margaret Thatcher withdrew from Conservative Party leadership
contest and was replaced by John Major.

David Owen disbanded Social Democratic Party due to lack of support.

Poll tax implemented as Community Charge in England. Anti-poll tax march in London turned into a riot.

Brian Keenan, one of several Western hostages held by militant Islamic groups in Beirut, freed after 1,597 days in captivity.

GATT (General Agreement on Tariffs and Trade) signed by 96 nations.

Operation Desert Shield: military operation by US and UN Allies in Kuwait to deter further Iraqi attacks on Kuwait after the Iraqi invasion of Kuwait (2 August).

George Carey made archbishop of Canterbury.

Channel Tunnel excavation teams from English and French sides met in the middle.

1991

The government replaced the Community Charge with a new Council Tax, based on property values.

British hostages in Beirut released by Islamic fundamentalist group Hezbollah: John McCarthy (August) and Terry Waite (November).

Gulf War began with operation Desert Storm: massive air bombardment of Iraqi forces in Kuwait by British, American and Saudi forces (17 January); land war began 24 February, and Iraq capitulated after 100-hour conflict.

Czech-born British publisher Robert Maxwell drowned at sea: his publishing empire collapsed with massive debts.

Deaths: the actress Dame Peggy Ashcroft; the ballerina Dame Margot Fonteyn; the film director Sir David Lean; the novelist Graham Greene; the rock star Freddie Mercury.

1992

Abolition of the Community Charge.

Britain forced to withdraw from the ERM (September).

Education Act for England and Wales.

General election won by the Conservatives (8 April). Neil Kinnock resigned as Labour Party leader; John Smith elected to succeed him.

Prince Charles and Diana the Princess of Wales announced their separation. Windsor Castle badly damaged by fire.

Privatization of the coal industry.

Deaths: actors Denholm Elliot and Robert Morley; artist Francis Bacon; comedians Benny Hill and Frankie Howerd.

1993

European Union inaugurated as Maastricht Treaty came into force.

Inauguration of the Single European Market.

John Major replaced Norman Lamont with Kenneth Clarke as
Chancellor of the Exchequer in a Cabinet reshuffle.

Ratification of the Treaty of Maastricht, providing a timebetable for
European political, economic and monetary union (July).

Government admitted to clandestine meetings with the IRA (November); Downing Street Declaration on Northern Ireland by John
Major and Albert Reynolds, Irish taoiseach, opened the way to all-party talks (December).

Betty Boothroyd became first woman Speaker of the House of
Commons.

Buckingham Palace opened to the public. Queen Elizabeth II agreed
to pay tax on private income.

The oil tanker *Braer* ran aground off Shetland.

Deaths: actress Audrey Hepburn; author, composer and critic Anthony
Burgess; writer Sir William Golding.

1994

IRA announced cease-fire in Northern Ireland, opening way for political
settlement (August); Loyalists announced cease-fire (October);
peace talks began between government and Sinn Fein (December).

John Smith, leader of Labour Party died; Tony Blair was elected to
replace him.

Queen Elizabeth II visited Russia.

National Lottery began (November). Sunday shopping introduced in
England.

Completion of a new opera house for Glyndebourne Festival Opera.

Channel Tunnel opened.

Deaths: actor Peter Cushing; film directors Derek Jarman and
Lindsay Anderson; philosopher Sir Karl Popper; playwright John
Osborne; television dramatist Dennis Potter; writer and historian Sir
Harold Acton; the writer Elias Canetti.

Index

Marlborough, John Churchill, Duke of 84, 85, 86, 87
Marlowe, Christopher 64
Marne, Battle of the 167
marriage, non-religious 127
Married Women's Property Act 150
Marshal, William, Earl of Pembroke 32
Marshall Plan 191
Marshal Rebellion 32
Marston Moor, Battle of 71
'Martin Marprelate' 63
Martinique 116
Marx, Karl 134, 150
Mary Celeste 145
Mary, Queen 154, 155, 195
Mary I 53, 58, 59, 83
Mary II 75, 78, 81
Mary of Guise 58, 59
Mary of Lorraine 55
Mary of Modena 78, 81
Mary Queen of Scots 56, 57, 59, 60, 61, 63
Maryland 69
Marylebone Cricket Club *see* MCC
Mary Rose 56, 212
Masefield, John 179, 206
Maserfeld, Battle of 12
Masham, Lady Abigail 91
Mason, James 213
Mason, John 69
Mason, Sir Josiah 125, 146
Masonic Lodge 88
Massachusetts 67; Bay Company 68
Master of the King's Musick 68, 175
Master of the Queen's Musick 195, 210
Masulipatam, Battle of 97
Matabele War 155
maternity benefit 166
Mathews, Admiral Thomas 92
Matilda (Maud) 26, 27, 28
Matthew, Jessie 212
Mauritius 116, 206
Mawson, Douglas 166
Maxton, James 180
Maxwell, James Clerk 140, 142, 143
Maxwell, Robert 216
mayor, first woman 163
Maze Prison 212
MCC (Marylebone Cricket Club) 107, 119; tour of South Africa 207
Meal Tub Plot 79
Meath 15
Medawar, Sir Peter 201
Medway, Battle of the 7
Meerut 137
Meikle, Andrew 106

Melbourne, Lord 126, 127, 128, 130, 134
Melrose Abbey 27
menachinite 108
Menai suspension bridge 123
mercerising 134
Mercia 11, 12, 13, 14, 17, 18
Merciless Parliament 44
Mercury, Freddie 216
Meredith, George 140, 164
Merit, Order of 160
Mermaid Theatre 199
Mersey tunnels 152, 181
Merton, Battle of 16
Merton College 34
Messina, Battle of *see* Cape Passero
Messines Ridge 170
Metaphysical Society 144
Meteorological Office 134
Methodist movement 91, 93, 180
Methuen, Lord 158
Methuen Treaty 85
Methven, Battle of 37
Metropolitan Police Force 124
Metropolitan Railway 141, 143, 161
Miani, Battle of 131
Milan Decree 115
Mildenhall Treasure 187
mile 64
Military Cross 168
Mill, John Stuart 140
Miller, Jonathan 201
Milne, A[lan] A[lexander] 177, 197
Milton, John 77, 78
Minden, Battle of 97
miners' strike 166, 176, 209, 213
Mini 200
mini cabs 201
minimum wage 166
Ministry of: Agriculture, Fisheries and Food 153; 'All the Talent' 114; Information 184
Minoan Script B 194
Minorca 86, 87, 96, 99, 105, 106, 111, 113
Minot, Laurence 41
Minto, Lord 157, 162
Mise of Amiens 34
Mississippi Scheme 88
Miss World contest 194
Modder River, Battle of 158
Model English Parliament 36
Mogadishu 185
Monck, George, Duke of Albemarle 74, 75
money orders 109
Monmouth, Duke of 79, 80
Monmouth, Battle of 103
Monmouth's Rebellion 80